Mastery Learning

Theory and Practice

**Edited by
James H. Block**

**With selected papers by
Peter W. Airasian
Benjamin S. Bloom
John B. Carroll**

HOLT, RINEHART AND WINSTON, INC.
*New York • Chicago • San Francisco • Atlanta
Dallas • Montreal • Toronto • London • Sydney*

In Memoriam

WILLIAM JOHN BLOCK

Viet Nam

(1947-1968)

PREFACE

One of the most powerful ideas beginning to shape educational views and practices is mastery learning. It assumes that all, or almost all, students can learn well and suggests explicit classroom procedures whereby all (up to 95 per cent) can achieve to high levels. Few recent ideas have produced more dramatic positive effects on student learning or generated more interest and school-based research than mastery learning.

This book brings together for the first time the basic mastery ideas and the relevant supporting research. The volume consists of two major parts. In Part One, a collection of articles focuses on both the theory behind mastery learning and the operating procedures required to implement an effective mastery strategy in a course, subject, or even an entire curriculum. Part Two presents an extensive annotated bibliography of mastery learning research. Studies bearing on the major mastery learning variables and those describing various successful mastery strategies have been abstracted. This arrangement is designed so that teachers, administrators, curriculum-makers, and researchers can draw some important implications from the data presented, pose some major questions, and suggest possible future research and new strategies.

Over the years educators have become convinced that only a few students can learn what we have to teach. Hopefully, the ideas and findings presented here will reverse this conviction.

*   *   *   *

This book could not have been completed without the assistance of many persons. I would like to thank Kenneth M. Collins, Mildred E. Kersh, Hogwon Kim, Christopher Modu, Kay Torshen, Robert Wise, and William J. Wright for their aid in abstracting some of the relevant mastery learning research. Special acknowledgments are due to John B. Carroll for his kind permission to reprint one of his papers and to Peter W. Airasian for his contributions to the Bibliography and his preparation of one of the mastery learning papers. Special recognition is also extended to Mrs. Ellen Hershey for her help in editing the manuscript and to Robert Zvolensky for his aid in preparing the manuscript for publication.

Finally, I would like to express my deepest gratitude to Benjamin S. Bloom and to my wife, Susan, for their many contributions to all aspects of the volume. It was under Dr. Bloom's direction and with his encouragement that I first began to assemble the book. In addition to contributing abstracts and a specially prepared paper, he read and commented on earlier manuscripts. Susan provided encouragement throughout the writing. She also typed and helped edit, proof-read, and prepare the final manuscript.

J. H. B.

October, 1970

TABLE OF CONTENTS

PART ONE

SELECTED PAPERS

ON

MASTERY LEARNING

Chapter 1

INTRODUCTION TO
MASTERY LEARNING: THEORY AND PRACTICE

James H. Block

American education is approaching a critical period in its
history. Despite great advances in knowledge about student learning and the investment of tremendous amounts of time, effort, and
money, our schools still have not moved very far toward the goal
of increased learning for all students. Present policies and practices continue to reproduce the same normal achievement distribution in the learning of classroom after classroom of students
that was produced in the learning of the students' parents and
perhaps grandparents. Thus the schools continue to provide successful and rewarding learning experiences for only about one-third
of our learners.

Recent research clearly suggests we can no longer afford to
allow one, let alone a majority, of our students face ten to twelve
long years of unsuccessful and unrewarding school learning experiences. Such experiences limit an individual's chances for economic survival and security in the world of work. He is likely to
acquire neither the basic skills nor the interests and attitudes
required to obtain and/or maintain a job which can ensure him a
decent standard of living. Such experiences also jeopardize the
individual's psychological well-being. The evidence indicates a
strong, perhaps causal, link between a pupil's history of school
learning success or failure and his personality development (See
Chapter 2). A student's inability to meet the school's learning

requirements tends to cause the development of a negative self-concept in minimally the academic arena. Further, for about 20 per cent of all students, the repeated frustration, humiliation, and despair engendered by their inability to meet these requirements may cause mental health problems.

Mastery learning (Bloom, 1968) offers a powerful new approach to student learning which can provide almost all students with the successful and rewarding learning experiences now allowed to only a few. It proposes that all or almost all students can master what they are taught. Further, it suggests procedures whereby each student's instruction and learning can be so managed, within the context of ordinary group-based classroom instruction, as to promote his fullest development. Mastery learning enables 75 to 90 per cent of the students to achieve to the same high level as the top 25 per cent learning under typical group-based instructional methods. It also makes student learning more efficient than conventional approaches. Students learn more material in less time. Finally, mastery learning produces markedly greater student interest in and attitude toward the subject learned than usual classroom methods.

HISTORY OF MASTERY LEARNING

Although effective mastery strategies have been developed only recently, the idea of learning for mastery is quite old. As early as the 1920's there were at least two major attempts to produce mastery in students' learning. One was the Winnetka Plan of Carleton Washburne and his associates (1922); the other was an approach developed by Professor Henry C. Morrison (1926) at the University of Chicago's Laboratory School.

These approaches shared many major features. First, mastery was defined in terms of particular educational objectives each student was expected to achieve. The objectives were cognitive for Washburne and cognitive, affective, and even psychomotor for Morrison. Second, instruction was organized into well-defined learning units. Each unit consisted of a collection of learning materials systematically arranged to teach the desired unit objectives (Washburne) or objective (Morrison). Third, complete mastery of each unit was required of students before proceeding to the next. This feature was especially important in the Winnetka Plan because the units tended to be sequenced so that the learning of each unit built upon prior learning.

Fourth, an ungraded, diagnostic-progress test was administered at the completion of each unit to provide feedback on the adequacy of the student's learning. This test either indicated unit

mastery, and thus reinforced his learning or it highlighted the material he still needed to master. Fifth, on the basis of this diagnostic
information, each student's original instruction was supplemented
with appropriate learning correctives so that he could complete his
unit learning. In the Winnetka Plan, primarily self-instructional
practice materials were used, although the teacher occasionally
tutored individuals or small groups. In Morrison's approach a
variety of correctives were used - - for example, reteaching,
tutoring, restructuring the original learning activities, and redir-
ecting student study habits. Finally, time was used as a variable
in individualizing instruction and thereby in fostering student learning mastery. Under the Winnetka Plan student learning was self-
paced - - each student was allowed all the time he needed to master a unit. Under Morrison's method each student was allowed the
learning time his teacher required to bring all or almost all students to unit mastery.

While especially Morrison's method was popular into the
1930's, eventually the idea of mastery learning disappeared due
primarily to the lack of the technology required to sustain a successful strategy. The idea did not resurface until the late 1950's
and early 1960's as a corollary of programed instruction. A basic
idea underlying programed instruction was that the learning of any
behavior, no matter how complex, rested upon the learning of a
sequence of less-complex component behaviors (Skinner, 1954).
Theoretically, therefore, by breaking a complex behavior down
into a chain of component behaviors and by ensuring student mastery of each link in the chain, it would be possible for any student
to master   even the most complex skills.

Programed instruction operationalized this theory as follows.
The criterion behavior was analyzed into a hierarchy of component
behaviors. Each component behavior was then presented in the
basic programed learning unit, the instructional frame. At a
frame's completion, the pupil responded to a simple diagnostic
question designed to indicate mastery or non-mastery of the behavior presented, and he was given immediate feedback on the adequacy
of his response. If his response was correct, his learning was
reinforced and he proceeded to the next frame (i. e. , behavior).
If incorrect, his error was immediately corrected so that misunder-
standings were not propagated.

Programed instruction seemed so promising that by the mid-
1960's there were major attempts to develop entire programed
instructional curricula. Two well-known examples were the Individually Prescribed Instruction (IPI) project at Pittsburgh (Glaser,
1968) and Stanford's Computer Assisted Instruction (CAI) project
(Atkinson, 1968; Suppes, 1966). The former program was designed
to teach arithmetic, reading, and science for grades K - 6 while

the latter focused on arithmetic and reading. Both approaches
broke the subjects into a sequence of major cognitive objectives
and developed programed learning units for each objective. Un-
like programed instruction, however, all students did not proceed
through the same programed lessons. Each pupil's learning progress was constantly monitored, and, on the basis of his present
and past performance, learning lessons were tailored to fit his
particular needs.

Programed instruction worked very well for some students,
especially those who required small learning steps, drill, and
frequent reinforcement, but it was not effective for all or almost
all students. Thus while programed instruction provided a valuable tool to help some students to attain mastery, it did not provide a useful mastery learning model.

A useful model was found, however, in John B. Carroll's
"Model of School Learning" (1963; See Chapter 3). Essentially
this was a conceptual paradigm which outlined the major factors
influencing student success in school learning and indicated how
these factors interacted. The model stemmed in part from Carroll's
earlier work in foreign language learning. Here he had found that
a student's aptitude for a language predicted not only the level to
which he learned in a given time, but also the amount of time he
required to learn to a given level. Rather than viewing aptitudes
as indexing the level to which a student could learn, therefore,
Carroll defined aptitudes as measuring the amount of time required
to learn a task to a given criterion level under ideal instructional
conditions. In its simplest form, his model proposed that if each
student was allowed the time he needed to learn to some level and
he spent the required learning time, then he could be expected to
attain the level. However, if the student was not allowed enough
time, then the degree to which he could be expected to learn was
a function of the ratio of the time actually spent in learning to the
time needed:

$$\text{Degree of Learning } = \text{ f} \left(\frac{\text{time actually spent}}{\text{time needed}} \right)$$

The full Carroll model conceived of school learning as
consisting of a series of distinct learning tasks. In each task the
student proceeded ". . . from ignorance of some specified fact or
concept to knowledge or understanding of it or. . . from incapability
of performing some act to capability of performing it" (Carroll,
1963, p 723). The model proposed that under typical school learning conditions, the time spent and the time needed were functions

of certain characteristics of the individual and his instruction.
The time spent was determined by the amount of time the student
was willing to spend actively involved in the learning (i.e., his
perseverance) and the total learning time he was allowed. The
learning time each student required was determined by his aptitude
for the task, the quality of his instruction, and his ability to understand the instruction. Quality of instruction was defined in terms
of the degree to which the presentation, explanation, and ordering
of the learning task's elements approached the optimum for each
learner. The ability to understand instruction represented the
student's ability to generally profit from the instruction and was
closely identified with general intelligence. The model proposed
that the quality of the student's instruction and his ability to
understand it interacted to extend the time he needed for task mastery beyond that normally required by his aptitude for the task.
If both the quality of his instruction and his ability to understand
it were high, then he would require little or no additional learning
time. However, if they were both low, then he would require much
additional time. The full Carroll model can be summarized as
follows:

$$\text{Degree of Learning} = f \left(\frac{\text{1. Time Allowed} \quad \text{2. Perseverance}}{\text{3. Aptitude} \quad \text{4. Quality of Instruction}} \atop \text{5. Ability to Understand Instruction} \right)$$

It was Bloom (1968; See Chapter 4) who transformed this
conceptual model into an effective working model for mastery
learning. If aptitudes were predictive of the rate at which, and
not necessarily the level to which, a student could learn a given
task, it should have been possible to fix the degree of learning
expected of students at some mastery level and to systematically
manipulate the relevant instructional variables in Carroll's model
such that all or almost all students attained it. Bloom argued that
if students were normally distributed with respect to aptitude for
a subject and if they were provided uniform instruction in terms
of quality and learning time, then achievement at the subject's
completion would be normally distributed. Further the relationship between aptitude and achievement would be high. This situation can be represented as follows:

Uniform Instruction
Per Learner

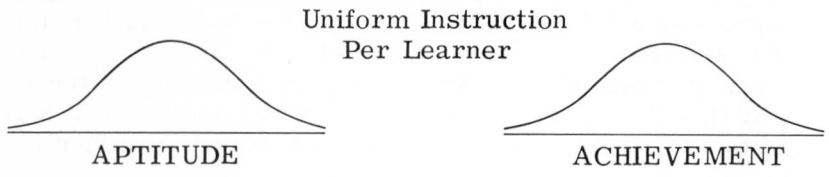

APTITUDE   ACHIEVEMENT

However, if students were normally distributed on aptitude but
each learner received optimal quality of instruction and the learning
time he required, then a majority of students could be expected to
attain mastery. There would be little or no relationship between
aptitude and achievement. This situation can be represented as
follows:

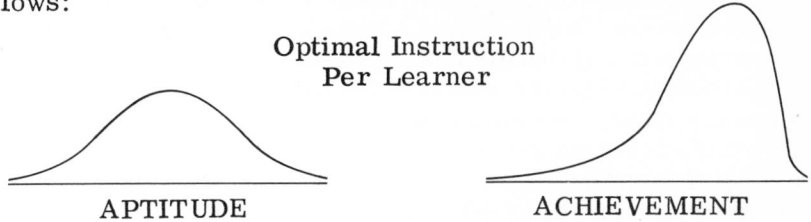

Optimal Instruction
Per Learner

APTITUDE   ACHIEVEMENT

The mastery learning strategy Bloom proposed to implement
these ideas was designed for use in the classroom where the time
allowed for learning is relatively fixed. Mastery was defined in
terms of a specific set of major objectives (content and cognitive
behaviors) the student was expected to exhibit by a subject's completion. The subject was then broken into a number of smaller
learning units (e.g., two weeks' instruction) and the unit objectives
were defined whose mastery was essential for mastery of the major
objectives. The instructor taught each unit using typical group-
based methods, but supplemented this instruction with simple feed-
back/correction procedures to ensure that each student's unit
instruction was of optimal quality. The feedback devices were
brief, diagnostic (formative) tests administered at the units'
completion. Each test covered all of a particular unit's objectives
and thus indicated what each student had or had not learned from
the unit's group-based instruction. Supplementary instructional
correctives were then applied to help the student overcome his
unit learning problems before the group instruction continued.

This approach to mastery learning represented a great advance over previous strategies in two important respects. First,
the feedback instruments were much improved. Their improvement
was attributable in part to the greater precision with which the
structure of the learning units could be described. The work of
Gagné (1968), Bloom et al. (1956) and others had provided procedures and categories for describing the unit's structure in terms
of its constituent elements (new content to be learned and the cognitive processes to be used in learning that content) and the inter-
relationships among elements. These structural descriptions
provided an excellent blue print from which the diagnostic instruments could be built. The feedback instruments' improvement was
also attributable to a major evaluation breakthrough called formative evaluation (Airasian, 1969; See Chapter 6). Formative evalua-

tion was designed to be an integral part of the teaching-learning
process and to provide continuous feedback to both the teacher and
the student regarding the process' on-going effectiveness. This
information enabled the continual modification of the process so
that each student could attain mastery.

Second, this strategy employed a greater variety of instructional correctives (See Chapter 5) than previous approaches. The
strategy assumed that quality of instruction could best be defined
in terms of a) the clarity and appropriateness of the instructional
cues for each pupil,   b) the amount of active participation in and
practice of the learning allowed each student, and c) the amount
and variety of reinforcements available to each learner. Under
the typical group-based instructional situation of one teacher to 30
students, it was unlikely that the quality of instruction was optimal
for all students. The sole function of the correctives was to provide each student with the instructional cues and/or the active
participation and practice and/or the amount and type of reinforcements he required to complete his unit learning. For these purposes, the following correctives were used: small-group study
sessions, individualized tutoring, alternative learning materials
(additional textbooks, workbooks, programed instruction, audio-
visual methods, and academic games), and reteaching. The small-
group sessions and the individualized tutoring, for example, added
an important personal-social component to each student's learning
not typically found in large-group instruction. The workbooks and
programed instruction provided the student with the drill he may
have required.

ABOUT THIS BOOK

In the three years since publication of Bloom's ideas, extensive mastery learning research has been carried out both here and
abroad. Successful strategies have been easily and inexpensively
implemented at all levels of education and in subjects ranging from
arithmetic to philosophy to physics. Mastery approaches have been
used for samples of up to 32,000 students and have been found to
work equally well in classrooms with one teacher to 20 students or
in those with one teacher to 70 students.

The results from approximately 40 major studies carried out
under actual school conditions have already been mentioned at the
chapter's outset. In general, three-fourths of the students learning
under mastery conditions have achieved to the same high standards
as the top one-fourth learning under conventional, group-based
instructional conditions. In studies where a strategy has been re-
fined and replicated, 90 per cent of the mastery learning students

have achieved as well as the top 20 per cent of the non-mastery
learning students. Mastery learning students also have exhibited
markedly greater interest in and attitudes toward the subject
learned compared to non-mastery learning students. Such dramatic
cognitive and affective outcomes suggest that mastery learning
cannot be ignored in the planning of future educational practice.

This book brings together the basic mastery learning ideas
and the related research findings so that they may be shared by
interested teachers, administrators, curriculum makers and
researchers. Although much mastery learning research is
presently underway, the findings reported are as up to date as
possible. The book consists of two major parts. In Part One a
series of selected papers on various aspects of mastery learning
are presented. One of the strongest arguments for mastery learning is its capacity to ensure each student a history of successful
and rewarding school learning experiences and thus to shape
positive affective development. In Chapter 2 Benjamin S. Bloom
examines the affective consequences of school achievement under
the present educational system. He traces the process by which
this sytem destroys a sizeable number of students' interest in
learning, creates negative attitude toward the school and the self,
and infects a number of students with mental health problems.
In Chapter 3, John B. Carroll reviews his "Model of School Learning, " relates the model's variables to the idea of mastery learning
and discusses the problems of measuring these variables. An
adapted version of Bloom's original formulation of the mastery
learning idea is presented in Chapter 4.

Chapters 5 and 6 turn away from mastery learning theory and
focus on the practical problem of implementing an effective strategy
for a course, subject, or entire curriculum. In Chapter 5, the
editor summarizes the major operating procedures which have
been found to be most useful in past successful strategies. Topics
such as defining and measuring mastery, selecting subjects for
mastery learning, using formative evaluation, selecting learning
correctives, allocating instructional time, and orienting students
are considered.

To individualize instruction within the context of ordinary
group-based instruction, mastery learning strategies rely heavily
on the constant flow of feedback information to both the teacher and
the learner. Two types of evaluation are used - - formative and
summative. In Chapter 6, Peter W. Airasian discusses the role
of evaluation in mastery learning and the properties, uses, and
construction of summative and formative instruments.

Part Two of the book contains an extensive annotated bibliography of the relevant empirical mastery learning research.
Studies bearing on the major mastery learning variables and papers

describing various successful mastery strategies have been abstracted. Each abstract is quite detailed and is indexed to indicate its relevance to one or more of the following categories: aptitudes and rate of learning, ability to understand instruction, quality of instruction, perseverance, time as a variable in attaining mastery, affective consequences of school learning, and use of mastery concepts and strategies. To facilitate use of the Bibliography, brief summaries have been prepared of all the research for each category. The reader will find the Bibliography of greatest use if he first reads the summaries and then the abstracts for the categories of particular interest.

A FINAL NOTE

Mastery learning offers exciting possibilities for those who would use and/or study it. Teachers will find as they examine the ideas and findings presented here that mastery learning strategies provide an efficient and effective means to transform their original group instruction into instruction of optimal quality per learner. Mastery procedures, therefore, will enable each teacher to make his great investment of time and effort in the group instruction pay-off in terms of increased learning for almost all, rather than just some, students.

Administrators will find that mastery learning methods are an easy and inexpensive means of adapting present instructional methods and materials to the needs and characteristics of all learners so as to promote the students' fullest development. By using mastery approaches administrators can greatly shift their schools' entire achievement distribution upwards. They can ensure each student is provided with those skills, interests, and attitudes which will encourage him to complete secondary school and to seek the advanced learning and training (e.g., higher education) our society increasingly demands of new workers. They can also ensure that each student acquires a history of successful learning experiences that will help shape his self-confidence and immunize him against mental illness.

Finally, curriculum-makers and researchers will find mastery learning rich in opportunities for future development and research efforts. Three especially promising areas for further work lie in the development of mastery learning curricula, the development of even more efficient and effective correction procedures, and the examination of the relationship between individual differences and student learning.

Typically past mastery learning strategies have been implemented in single subjects. The greatest pay-off in terms of student development, however, is likely to result from the implementation of an entire mastery learning curricula. In building such curricula, curriculum-makers might consider the possibilities of expanding already existing strategies (See the Bibliography - - Kim et al., 1969, 1970 - - for a good example of this approach.)

Undoubtedly, the development of mastery learning curricula will also entail the construction of even better strategies than presently exist. A key to the construction of such strategies will be the development of more efficient and effective correction procedures. At present there is no way to go from an incorrect formative test response to the prescription of the particular corrective or combination of correctives a particular student may need to overcome his errors. Much additional research is needed on the kinds of correctives best suited for certain types of students and those most useful in the classroom.

As progressively better correction procedures are developed, the relationship between individual differences and student learning should be critically examined. Past mastery learning research suggests that the relationship may be largely an artifact of present instructional practices (Block, 1970; Kim et al., 1969). The findings demonstrate that if no attempt is made to optimize the quality of each student's classroom instruction, then individual differences in student entry resources (e.g., I.Q., aptitudes, and previous learning) are reflected in their achievement. However, if the quality is made optimal by means of supplementary feedback/correction procedures, then the differences are not reflected in student achievement.

For many years individual differences have been used to justify the fact that all cannot learn and that some can learn better than others. If the preceding findings are replicated, however, is it not possible that individual differences have been used as a scapegoat for ineffective instruction?

REFERENCES

Airasian, Peter W. "Formative Evaluation Instruments: A Construction and Validation of Tests to Evaluate Learning Over Short Time Periods." Unpublished Ph.D. dissertation, University of Chicago, 1969.

Atkinson, Richard C. "Computer-based Instruction in Initial Reading," In Proceedings of the 1967 Invitational Conference on Testing Problems. Princeton, New Jersey: Educational Testing Service.

REFERENCES CONTINUED

Block, James H. "The Effects of Various Levels of Performance
on Selected Cognitive, Affective, and Time Variables." Unpublished Ph.D. dissertation, University of Chicago, 1970.

Bloom, Benjamin S. "Learning for Mastery," UCLA - CSEIP
Evaluation Comment, 1, No. 2 (1968).

Bloom, Benjamin S., et al. (eds.). Taxonomy of Educational
Objectives, Handbook I: Cognitive Domain. New York:
David McKay Co., Inc., 1956.

Carroll, John B. "A Model of School Learning," Teachers College
Record, 64 (1963), 723-33.

Gagné, Robert M. The Conditions of Learning. New York: Holt,
Rinehart, and Winston, Inc., 1965.

Glaser, Robert. "Adapting the Elementary School Curriculum to
Individual Performance," In Proceedings of the 1967 Invita-
tional Conference on Testing Problems. Princeton, New
Jersey: Educational Testing Service.

Kim, Hogwon, et al. A Study of the Bloom Strategies for Mastery
Learning. Seoul: Korean Institute for Research in the
Behavioral Sciences, 1969. (In Korean.)

Kim, Hogwon, et al. The Mastery Learning Project in the Middle
Schools. Seoul: Korean Institute for Research in the Behavioral Sciences, 1970. (In Korean.)

Morrison, H. C. The Practice of Teaching in the Secondary School.
Chicago: University of Chicago Press, 1926.

Skinner, B. F. "The Science of Learning and the Art of Teaching,"
Harvard Educational Review, 24 (1954), 86-97.

Suppes, P. "The Uses of Computers in Education," Scientific
American, 215 (1966), 206-221.

Washburne, Carleton W. "Educational Measurements as a Key
to Individualizing Instruction and Promotions," Journal of
Educational Research, 5 (1922), 195-206.

Chapter 2

AFFECTIVE CONSEQUENCES OF SCHOOL ACHIEVEMENT*

Benjamin S. Bloom, University of Chicago

For young people in the United States, school attendance is a dominant feature in their lives for a 10 to 16 year period. During this time, the student devotes at least a 40 hour week (for nine months out of the year) to school attendance, homework, and related activities. Thus, annually, the typical student spends about 1500 hours on school and related activities. The student who completes secondary school has devoted almost 20,000 hours to school. It is the way in which the student and the school use this tremendous amount of time that determines school achievement and the affective consequences of such achievement.

During this long period of time, in some of the most impressionable stages of individual development, the student is being taught at least two courses of study or curricula. One is the explicit curriculum of the school, while the other is a curriculum implicit in the interactions of persons within the school.

Most visible is the explicit curriculum the student is expected to learn. It includes the reading, mathematics, science, literature, social studies, and other school subjects he is taught. This

*This article will also appear in Advances in Educational Psychology 2. Edited by Varma and Pringle. London, England: University of London Press, Ltd. (In preparation.)

curriculum may be of great importance to the learner because of the competence he develops, the interests and attitudes he acquires, and the career opportunities which are made available to those who learn it well. Undoubtedly, it may include important as well as trivial content. It may be taught well or it may be taught poorly. It may be meaningful to some students and it may seem meaningless and a waste of time to others. Some of it may be remembered and used repeatedly by the learners, while some of it may be forgotten quickly and discarded. The explicit curriculum is visible, it is documented in many ways, and most of the resources and personnel of the schools are dedicated to the students' learning of it.

The second curriculum is not so clearly visible. This is the implicit curriculum which is taught and learned differently by each student. This is the curriculum which teaches each student who he is in relation to others. It may also teach each person his place in the world of people, of ideas, and of activities. While the student may learn this curriculum more slowly than the other, it is likely that he will not be able to forget it as easily as he can forget the details of history, the rules of grammar, or the specifics of any subject of study in the explicit curriculum.

While there are many ways of viewing the implicit curriculum, we will confine ourselves in this paper to those aspects of it which are most clearly related to the effects of the judgmental processes in the school. It is because of the pervasive use of relative judgments about students in the school that some aspects of the implicit curriculum manifest themselves and can be studied quite directly. Other aspects of the implicit curriculum may be examined only through case studies of individuals or by more deep seated and complex psychological and anthropological methods of study.

In the many hours of school attendance and school work pointed up in the opening paragraph, there are few hours in which the student is not judged (relative to others) by his teachers, peers, family, and others. Likewise, there are few school hours in which the student is not judging himself against the standards set by himself, the teacher, or peers and his family. Nowhere else in his career as a worker, as a member of a family, as a citizen, or as a person engaging in leisure time activities will he be judged so frequently by others and, it is possible, by himself. In most of these post school activities, the individual is expected to meet some minimal standards of competence or behavior; if he does so, he is usually not judged in more detailed terms. For example, the majority of workers are expected to meet some minimal standard of work - - usually relatively low - - and are only rarely judged relative to others.

In school, the likelihood is that each student will be judged many times each day in terms of his adequacy relative to others in his class, group, or school. No matter how well he does, if others do better, he must come to know it and to place himself accordingly. No matter how poorly he does, if others do less well, he also comes to know it. Obviously, these relative judgments arise because almost all of the student's school learning is as a member of a group - - probably of the order of 25 to 35 members. Also, these judgments are made so frequently because the schools have for so long stressed competition as a primary motivational technique. Only rarely are the judgments in school based on some criterion of adequate work or learning independent of relative performance among the students. Relative rather than absolute norms are the bases for most judgments (Bormuth, 1970; Glaser and Nitko, 1970; Popham and Husek, 1969).

Furthermore, because of the consistency of the learning tasks from one year to another and the sequential nature of many of the tasks in a subject or field, the student who moves from one task to the next tends to remain in much the same position relative to other students (providing he remains with the same group of students or with representatives of much the same sample of students) from one year to the next. The increasing stability of marks and test performance are well documented in the longitudinal research summarized by Bloom (1964), Hicklin (1962), and Payne (1963).

We are accustomed to the notion that courses and instruction in school are divided into subjects and time periods such as an academic year or term. However, we believe it possible to understand the affective consequences of school achievement more clearly if we consider the learning task as the basic unit. If we conceive of the typical learning task as requiring about six to eight hours of instruction or learning activity on the part of a student, we may then see that, in an academic year, a student may encounter about 200 separable learning tasks. And, over a 10-year period of school, he may encounter of the order of 2000 separable learning tasks.

However, in the student's perception, there are really not that many separable learning tasks - - that is, each one is not completely isolated from every other one in his view - - nor are they so isolated in the teacher's view. The student comes to perceive the learning tasks in a subject or course of study as all having somewhat the same characteristics.

The curriculum and textbook makers and the teacher attempt to organize learning tasks by subjects or fields of content and then arrange the learning tasks in a sequential or logical order. Thus, in third grade arithmetic, there may be about 25 learning tasks arranged in a sequence that someone believes appropriate from a logical, instructional, or learning point of view. Similarly, reading, language arts, science, social studies and so on, are also composed of learning tasks arranged in some order.

In studying a subject, then, the student encounters the first learning task in a series of such tasks. He is instructed as to what to do, he is provided with instructional material, he is expected to make the appropriate efforts, and he is judged by the teacher on how well he succeeds in this learning task. Typically the student may be given some quantitative index by the teacher such as a mark or grade on his achievement over the learning task. Frequently he may also be given some qualitative judgment or appraisal by the teacher on his work. In addition, the student may judge his own success on the task by inferring whether the teacher approves or disapproves of him and his work. The student may also infer how well he accomplished the task by the degree of confidence he has in the work he did, the questions he answered, or the procedures he used in responding to the task. However he comes to know it, the student has a rough idea of his accomplishment of the task.

INTEREST

If the student secures evidence that he did the first task superbly, he is likely to approach the next task in the series with a bit more enthusiasm and confidence. If he secures evidence that he did the first task very badly, he is likely to approach the next task in the series with somewhat less enthusiasm than he approached the first. And so the student progresses from task to task. For each task, he secures some simple judgment about the adequacy of his performance - - from the teacher, from himself, or both. For the most part, these judgments on each task are not made public, and a student may entertain the delusion that he is doing better or worse than he really is.

At various stages in a series of tasks, the grades or marks are made partly public - - at least to the parents. It is here that the student may have difficulty in reconciling the report of his marks with his own more private impressions of the adequacy of his performance on each of the tasks in the subject, especially if the mark is lower than he expected. At this point, he may believe the teacher was in error; that the test or other evidence on which the mark was based was not valid or fair; or that the teacher was unfair and/or does not like him. Since his reported marks are more public, they are likely to have a somewhat greater effect on the student than the more private day to day judgments about the adequacy of performance on each of the learning tasks in the series. And marks at the end of the term or year are likely to have an even greater effect than marks given at various stages during the term. In general, the more public and official the judgments (or marks) the greater the effect they are likely to have on the student's perception of his adequacy in the subject.

Over a long series of learning tasks of a particular type, the student comes to secure many judgments of his own performance and capability with this class of learning tasks. With some variations from task to task, and with many corrections imposed on his private judgments by the more public appraisals of his performance, he comes to see himself as highly capable with this type of task, moderate in capability, or low in capability. Since he is likely to be given one or more years of a particular type of task - - and probably on the order of 25 tasks of a particular type in a year - - he is forced sooner or later to accept some judgment about his capability with this group of learning tasks.

If the same type of learning task (e.g., arithmetic, reading, or social studies, and so on) is given for four to six years, the student may have experiences with on the order of 100 to 150 learning tasks of a particular type. Because of the similarity in the type of learning task; because of the sequential nature of many of these learning tasks; and because of the student's gradual structuring of his aspirations, approach to the tasks, and views of the task, there is likely to be high relationship between the adequacy-inadequacy of his performance over several years or terms. That is, the student gradually acquires a consistent performance as the tasks begin to accumulate in larger numbers.

As these performances and the student's perceptions of them accumulate and become more consistent, his motivations for the next tasks in the series take on a stable quality. If his performance has been adequate, he approaches the next task with confidence and assurance that he can do it well - - and he may even develop a desire for more such tasks. They are easy to do, they can be learned, and they may even be likeable tasks because they can be mastered, solved, learned, or overcome. If his performance has not been adequate over a number of tasks of a particular type, the student comes to believe in his inadequacy with respect to this type of learning. He approaches the next task in the series with marked reluctance. He expects the worst and is prepared for it. If his past experiences have been painful enough, the task is avoided, approached with little enthusiasm and, if anything, marked dislike. Where the student is convinced of his inadequacy, he finds no great energy to accomplish the next task, has little patience or perseverance when he encounters difficulties, and takes little care and thoroughness in accomplishing the task (White, 1959; Atkinson and Feather, 1966).

Interest in a subject or category of learning tasks may be defined behaviorally in terms of whether or not the individual would voluntarily engage in additional learning tasks of this type - -

if free to make such a choice. Interest may also be defined more subjectively in terms of the individual's liking, enthusiasm, positive view, preference, and desire. Here we are taking the position that the student's subjective feelings about a subject or set of learning tasks are influenced by his perceptions of his adequacy or inadequacy with such tasks. In turn, his perceptions of adequacy or inadequacy are based on his previous history with such tasks and especially the previous judgments about his learning of such tasks.

Studies on the relation between achievement and interest measures have been reported for various school subjects (Neale, 1969; Husén, 1967; Anttonen, 1969; Baraheni, 1962; Frandsen and Sessions, 1953; Wyman, 1924). In general, the relations are between +.20 and +.50, suggesting statistically, at least, that the relationships are most clear for extreme students on achievement (or interest).

In summary, each of the tasks in a series of learning tasks comes to take on a special meaning for the student which is related to his sense of adequacy in accomplishing previous tasks in the series. The student's confidence in himself with respect to the type of task is enhanced or reduced by his performance over the previous tasks. Eventually the student's prophecy for the next task in the series, based on his previous perceptions of success or failure, becomes fulfilled. Under extreme conditions, we can imagine individual students who resist accepting adequacy or inadequacy as their lot with this type of task, but even they cannot hold out forever.

We believe this general result will be found in each subject or type of learning experience. Through an accumulation of experience with learning tasks he perceives to be similar or in the same category, the student's interest gradually stabilizes, and he comes to view the next task in the series with disinterest, interest, or something in-between.

This view assumes that the definition of student learning adequacy or inadequacy is based on the local situation - - the school the student attends, the teachers' marking schemes, and the student's performance relative to other students in the same class. It is likely that for a few students, their perceptions of adequacy or inadequacy are based on a sibling-like rivalry with a few other students in the school or class, or with an actual sibling. Under these conditions, it may be catastrophic for a student to be slightly below his rival, while to be slightly above the rival may appear to him to be success. However, these are individual cases. For the most part, adequacy or inadequacy for most students is defined in terms of their standing in the upper or lower portion of the local distribution of marks.

Thus interest in a subject is largely a perceptual phenomena based on the way in which students classify learning tasks and on the judgments they make of the adequacy of their performance relative to the other students in the school or class they attend. What we are stating here has consequences for further efforts at learning the particular subject or type of learning tasks. Indications of inadequacy over a series of learning tasks are effective in foreclosing further motivation for this type of task. Such indications have important effects on career choice, choice of educational specialization, and even on the avocational use of a school subject or area of learning (Husén, 1967; Husén, 1969).

Success (or adequacy) in a school subject opens it up for further consideration and use. Failure (or inadequacy) in a school subject effectively closes it for further consideration. The system of grading and instruction operates to open doors for some students while effectively closing them for others - - and this system is independent of success or failure in any absolute sense. It is dependent on local definitions of success and failure.

In summary, we are postulating a causal relationship between clear indications of a student's adequacy or inadequacy in learning a particular type of learning task and his interest or disinterest in that type of learning task. Given freedom to continue learning more tasks in the series, a high proportion of those who perceive themselves as inadequate over the previous learning tasks in the series will avoid further learning tasks of this type. Similarly, a high proportion of those who perceive themselves as highly adequate will choose to learn more tasks of this type. However, with increasing age and maturity, those who perceive themselves as adequate will base their choices on the meaningfulness of the task and its relevance to their overall desires and plans for the future. Such students have many more possibilities open to them, and they will increasingly make decisions on other criteria than school success.

ATTITUDES

So far, we have been discussing a series of learning tasks which the student perceives as members of a single category. Here we considered the effect of a stabilizing picture of success or adequacy and failure or inadequacy on the interest or disinterest the student develops for this type of task and his willingness to voluntarily engage in more learning tasks of the same or related type (as perceived by the student).

If we then turn to the other learning tasks which the student is being given at the same time, we can also ask about the effect of evidence of adequacy or inadequacy. Thus, in a school year, the student may study as many as five school subjects and may encounter as many as 150 learning tasks. As he encounters each of these tasks, he has a sense of adequacy or inadequacy. These impressions are corroborated or altered by marks assigned by teachers at various marking periods. As these various indices accumulate, over many learning tasks and over several years, the student begins to generalize about his adequacy or inadequacy in school learning tasks. If his experiences are positive - - that is, the results are generally adequate - - he comes to have a positive attitude toward school and school learning. If the results are generally negative and his learning is regarded as inadequate by himself, his teacher, and his parents, he comes to have a negative attitude toward school and school learning.

By attitude we mean a general disposition to regard something in a positive or negative way. We are here treating attitudes as more general than interests. If the student develops a negative (or positive) attitude toward school it may include the subjects, the teachers and staff, and even the whole idea of school and school learning.

We believe that different amounts of failure (or success) may be needed for different students to develop this negative or positive attitude toward school. However, we believe that this is only a matter of degree, and that all individuals who accumulate sufficient experiences of failure (or sucess) will at some point develop negative or positive attitudes toward school.

Many studies have been done on the relation between school achievement and attitudes toward school (e.g., Flemming, 1925; Khan, 1969; Kurtz and Swenson, 1951; Michael, Baker, and Jones, 1964; and Russell, 1969). Especially for students who are extremes on school achievement, there is a relation between positive and negative attitudes and indications of adequacy or inadequacy in school achievement. It is evident in some of these studies that relatively strong attitudes have been developed in many students by the end of the elementary period of schooling.

The degree of certainty of attitude formation is likely to be much greater for the negative attitudes and repeated evidence of inadequacy than it is for the effects of repeated evidence of adequacy. While indications of success in school are likely to result in positive attitudes toward it, other variables may enter in to determine whether the school and school learning is viewed as positive and favorable (e.g., values of parents, peer group attitudes, meaningfulness of schooling for the individual's career aspirations, and so on).

Attitude toward school and school learning is much more generalized than interest in a specific subject or types of learning tasks. Interest is specific, and while it generalizes to a class of learning tasks, it need not extend beyond the members of the category. Attitude generalizes to the whole institution of the school,

to most of the school subjects, to the staff of the school, and even
to the students who attend the school. In effect, repeated evidence
of inadequacy in school makes the entire institution the source of
the individual's sense of inadequacy and he must avoid the institution or find some way of reducing the amount of pain it gives to him.
This he does by efforts of retreating, attacking, or minimizing the
school's effects on him. Such negative attitudes, if developed fully
enough, may have consequences for all later efforts to do school
learning or learning in any way related to schools.

SELF-CONCEPT

While there is a difference in generality between interests and
attitudes, as we have defined them, in both cases the object of the
affect is outside the individual. The student develops an interest
in something or he develops a disinterest in something. He
develops a positive attitude toward school and school learning or
he develops a negative attitude toward school and school learning.
However, if the process of adequate or inadequate appraisals with
regard to learning tasks is generalized over a large number of
tasks over a number of years, eventually the object of appraisal
for the student shifts from the subjects or the school to the self.
If the individual works and studies in an environment in which
the majority of learning tasks over a period of years are accompanied by self-appraisals and external appraisals as adequate, he
develops a general sense of adequacy - - at least in connection
with school activities. Similarly, if most of his encounters with
learning tasks are accompanied by appraisals of inadequacy, the
individual is likely to develop a deep sense of inadequacy - - at
least in connection with school activities.
While we recognize that some individuals may need more
successful-unsuccessful experiences before they come to accept a
particular view of themselves, we believe this is only a matter of
degree. Given a sufficient number of unsuccessful experiences,
almost everyone must eventually succumb to an acceptance of a
self-view which is negative or inadequate. Similarly, given enough
successful encounters with learning experiences,one must eventually come to a self-view which is positive or adequate.
We do not believe that a few successful or unsuccessful experiences have a major effect on the self-concept; in fact, it is
possible that occasional unsuccessful experiences which can be
turned by the individual into successful experiences may be of
special significance in strengthening his self-image. It is the
frequency and consistency of judgments of adequacy or inadequacy
over a period of years which has major effects on self-concept.

We do not know what level of objective success or failure will be interpreted by the individual as success or failure. But, in general, we believe that to be in the top third or top quarter of his class group (grades of A and B) over a number of years in a variety of school subjects is likely to be interpreted by the student as adequate or as success. Also, we believe to be in the bottom third or quarter of his class group (grades of D and F) over a number of years must leave the individual with a negative self-view - - at least in the academic area.

Torshen (1969) has summarized the studies showing relationships between self-concept and school achievement. While the correlation between <u>total</u> self-concept and school achievement is of the order of +.25, the correlation between <u>academic</u> self-concept and school achievement is about +.50. It is evident in these studies that the academic self-concept is relatively clearly defined by the end of the primary school period. These correlations indicate that for students at the extremes (upper and lower third) on academic achievement, the relationship between achievement and academic self-concept is very strong, with little overlap in academic self-concept between these extreme groups. That is, students in the lower third of the achievement distribution tend to have negative self-concepts while students in the upper third tend to have positive self-concepts.

It is probable that occasional individuals may take some comfort in the fact that a few members of their class are in even worse academic shape than they - - but this rationalization is probably of little comfort over a long period of time. So too, some individuals may be depressed that a few members of their class do slightly better than they, but again we believe that for students to be in the top third or quarter of their class will eventually be interpreted in a positive way.

It is the middle third or half of the students who may be least affected by the school insofar as self-concept may be concerned. They are given enough positive evidence of their adequacy to balance the negative evidence, or at least they can take some comfort that they are more adequate than a sizeable proportion of their peers. Undoubtedly, they must turn to other areas of activity and to other aspects of themselves to find more positive signs of their worth and adequacy.

In taking these views, we are assuming that each individual seeks desperately for some positive signs of his own adequacy and worth. If these indications are denied in one area, the individual must seek them in other areas. In the work of Sears (1963) in measuring self-concept, there are twelve areas in which an individual may appraise himself. Some of these, such as learning, school subjects, work habits, and relations with the teacher, may be clearly classified as relating to the student's academic self-concept. Others, having to do with self-appraisals with regard to athletics, relations with boys and girls, relations with others, and appearance, may be classified as relating to his non-academic self-concept. There is a low relationship between these two large categories of self-concept (about +.35), indicating that individuals who are high on one may or may not be high on the other. Some individuals who are low in academic self-concept may be high in non-academic self-concept and vice versa. It is likely that individuals who are low in both are in great difficulty, and this may be true for up to half of the students who are low in academic self-concept.

It is possible for some individuals who are low in academic self-concept to get considerable comfort from a positive non-academic self-concept. However, the academic self-concept is important in its own right as determining whether or not the individual will voluntarily engage in academic learning when he is free to do so or not. Also, a low academic self-concept increases the probability that an individual will have a generally negative self-concept.

We believe that the individual who is denied positive reassurance of his worth in school is impelled to seek such positive reassurance wherever he can find it. If society offers him opportunities for work which is satisfying and rewarding financially, as well as otherwise, the individual can find positive indications of self-worth here. However, in a highly developed society like the United States, negative indications of school achievement (including dropping out of school) are likely to provide serious barriers against securing skilled or higher occupational employment. Some individuals must turn to less socially approved areas (gangs, illicit activities, and so on) to find the rewards and self-approval denied them in school and school-related activities.

In summary, successful experiences in school are no guarantee of a generally positive self-concept, but they increase the probability that such will be the case. In contrast, unsuccessful experiences in school guarantee that the individual will develop a negative academic self-concept and increase the probability that he will have a generally negative self-concept. But the individual strives desperately to secure some assurance of his self-worth; if he is denied it in one area, he will search for it elsewhere. The likelihood of his finding it is considerably decreased by consistent lack of success in school.

MENTAL HEALTH

An individual develops a positive self regard and a strong ego

by continual evidence of his adequacy - - especially in early childhood and in the periods of latency (ages 6 - 11) and adolescence.
Since the school period (ages 6 - 18) occupies these latter two
periods, we regard continual evidence of success or failure in the
school as having major effects on the individual's mental health.
While mental health and self-concept cannot be sharply distinguished,
we may think of mental health as concerned more directly with ego
development, with reduction in general anxiety, and with the ability
to take stress and frustration with a minimum of debilitating affect.

There is considerable empirical support for relating the individual's perception of his adequacy in school learning to the development of related interests, attitudes, and self-concept. When we
turn to mental health, we must be more speculative because of the
difficulties in defining and measuring mental health and because of
the limited amount of research which directly relates adequacy in
school learning to mental health. Some support for these speculations may be drawn from a longitudinal study by Stringer and
Glidewell (1967) which related the academic progress of elementary
school pupils to indications of mental illness. A more recent
study by Torshen (1969) of the relation between teachers' grades,
self-concepts, and indications of mental health gives some further
support to these ideas. However, the crucial empirical test of
these hypotheses has not been done (at least to the writer's satisfaction.)

If the school environment provides the individual with evidence
of his adequacy over a number of years, especially in the first few
years of school supported by consistent success over the next four
or five years, we believe that this provides a type of immunization
against mental illness for an indefinite period of time. Such an
individual should be able to surmount crises and periods of great
stress without suffering too much. His own sense of adequacy and
his personal and technical skills (some learned in school) should
enable him to use realistic methods in surmounting these crisis
situations.

It is not likely that all students in the upper fourth or third of
their classes in school achievement will secure this ego strengthening from adequacy in school learning. However, we believe this
should be true for about two-thirds of the students in the upper third
of their classes (i.e., over 20 per cent of all students). We are
not quite sure why the other one-third should lack this immunization.
Probably some of this group are compulsive students who achieve
school success at great personal cost. Perhaps, also, some are
highly competitive students who make school grades and competition with others more central than the learning represented by
these grades. Perhaps, also, some are overly docile students who
lose independence by conforming overly much to the demands of adults

(parents, teachers, and so on) without developing their own personal goals.

At the other extreme are the bottom third of the students who
have been given consistent evidence of their inadequacy in the school
learning environment over a period of five to ten years. Such students rarely secure any positive reinforcement in the classroom
and are unlikely to secure positive rewards from teachers or parents. We would expect them to be infected with emotional difficulties arising from the rarity with which they can secure any
sense of adequacy in the school environment - - and especially in
the classroom. There must be an increasing spiral in which some
difficulty in learning at one point becomes exaggerated at a later
point, gradually producing a sense that there is nothing one can do
right in such a situation.

From this, we would expect that about two-thirds of the students in the bottom third of their classes (about 20 per cent of all
students) over a period of years should exhibit symptoms of acute
distress and alienation from the world of school and adults. Again,
we can only speculate about how and why some students can escape
from the infection likely to result from a deep sense of inadequacy
in school. Some students must be able to secure a strong and
positive sense of adequacy in their work, from their peers, from
their parents, and so on to compensate for the negative effects of
the school. Others may find it possible to reject their school
experiences as irrelevant to their own goals, or they may regard
the judgments of the school as unfair and thus escape from the
effect of what would otherwise be negative experiences and judgments.

For students at both the upper and the lower achievement
extremes, we would expect the effects of school experiences to be
most pronounced when the parents are most interested and concerned about the educational achievement of their children. When
the parents' educational aspirations for their children are high,
they will reward achievement and punish lack of achievement.
Under such conditions, the reward and punishment system of the
school is paralleled by the reward and punishment system of the
home. For such children the affective consequences of school
achievement should be far greater than when the home has a different basis for reward and punishment than does the school.

We would also expect the effects of failure in the cognitive
learnings in the school would be minimized when the school provides many types of learning and activities which have relatively
low relations to the cognitive learning (i.e., athletics, social
activities, art, music, vocational instruction, and so on). Under
such conditions, it is likely that a high proportion of students can
experience some degree of success in some school-related activ-

ities and thus escape a complete sense of failure in connection with school.

The speculations and hypotheses on the preceding pages may be derived from such work as White (1959) on competence motivation, Erickson (1963) on stages in development, and Bower (1962) in his review of research on mental health in education. In spite of the speculative nature of this section of the paper, the suggestive research already done, the theoretical work of child development specialists, and the experiences of psychiatric and psychological workers all give indications in the direction spelled out in this section of the paper. The extreme importance of this area for the individual and the society make it important that these speculations and hypotheses be the subject of more definitive research.

REFERENCES

Anttonen, R. G. "Longitudinal Study in Mathematics Attitude," Journal of Educational Research, 62 (1969), 467-71.

Atkinson, J. W. , and Feather, N. T. (eds.). A Theory of Achievement Motivation. New York: John Wiley & Sons, 1966.

Baraheni, M. N. "Inquiry into Attitudinal Concomitants of Success and Failure at School," Educational Research, 5 (1962), 63-68.

Bloom, B. S. Stability and Change in Human Characteristics. New York: John Wiley & Sons, 1964.

Bormuth, J. R. On the Theory of Achievement Test Items. Chicago: University of Chicago Press, 1970.

Bower, E. M. "Mental Health in Education," Review of Educational Research, 32 (1962), 441-54.

Engel, M. "The Stability of Self-concept in Adolescence," Journal of Abnormal and Social Psychology, 58 (1959), 211-15.

Erikson, E. H. Childhood and Society. New York: Norton, 1963.

Flemming, C. W. "A Detailed Analysis of Achievement in High School," Teachers College Contributions to Education, No. 196 (New York: Bureau of Publications, Teachers College, Columbia University, 1925), pp. 35-47.

Frandsen, A. N. , and Sessions, A. D. "Interests and School
    Achievement," Educational and Psychological Measurement,
    13 (1953), 94-101.

Glaser, R. , and Nitko, A. J. Measurement in Learning and
    Instruction. Pittsburgh: University of Pittsburgh, Research
    and Development Center, 1970.

Hicklin, William J. "A Study of Long-Range Techniques for Pre-
    dicting Patterns of Scholastic Behavior." Unpublished Ph.D.
    dissertation, University of Chicago, 1962.

Husén, T. (ed.). International Study of Educational Achievement in
    Mathematics: A Comparison of Twelve Countries, Vols. I
    and II. New York: John Wiley & Sons, 1967.

Husén, T. Talent, Opportunity and Career. Stockholm: Almquist
    and Wiksell, 1969.

Khan, S. B. "Affective Correlates of Academic Achievement,"
    Journal of Educational Psychology, 60 (1969), 216-21.

Kurtz, J. J. , and Swenson, E. J. "Student, Parent, and Teacher
    Attitude Toward Student Achievement in School," School
    Review, 59 (1951), 273-79.

Michael, W. B. , Baker, C., and Jones, R. A. " A Note Concern-
    ing the Predictive Validities of Selected Cognitive and Non-
    Cognitive Measures for Freshmen Students in a Liberal Arts
    College," Educational and Psychological Measurements, 24
    (1964), 373-75.

Neale, D. C. "The Role of Attitudes in Learning Mathematics,"
    The Arithmetic Teacher, 16 (1969), 631-40.

Payne, Margaret A. "The Use of Data in Curricular Decisions."
    Unpublished Ph.D. dissertation, University of Chicago, 1963.

Popham, W. J., and Husek, T. R. "Implications of Criterion-
    Referenced Measurement," Journal of Educational Measure-
    ment, 6 (1969), 1-9.

REFERENCES CONTINUED

Russell, I. L. "Motivation for School Achievement: Measurement
and Validation," Journal of Educational Research, 62 (1969),
263-66.

Sears, P. S. The Effect of Classroom Conditions on the Strength
of Achievement Motive and Work Output of Elementary School
Children. Cooperative Research Project No. OE 873.
Stanford, California: Stanford University, School of Education, 1963.

Stringer, L. A., and Glidewell, J. C. Early Detection of Emotional Illnesses in School Children. Final Report. St. Louis,
Missouri: St. Louis County Health Department, 1967.

Torshen, Kay. "The Relation of Classroom Evaluation to Students'
Self-Concepts and Mental Health." Unpublished Ph.D. dissertation, University of Chicago, 1969.

White, R. W. "Motivation Reconsidered: The Concept of Competence," Psychological Review, 66 (1959), 297-333.

Wyman, J. B. "On the Influence of Interest on Relative Success."
Unpublished Ph.D. dissertation, Stanford University, 1924.

Chapter 3

PROBLEMS OF MEASUREMENT RELATED TO
THE CONCEPT OF LEARNING FOR MASTERY*

John B. Carroll, Educational Testing Service

Teaching ought to be a simple matter since a good deal is
actually known about learning. To be sure, there are many things
which are not known about the learning process - its physiology,
among other things. But about the basics, quite a bit is known.
It is a known fact that students who are confident and well motivated,
provided with good basic intelligence and aptitude, and provided
with good instruction, can learn a fantastic amount in relatively
short periods of time. It is also a known fact that once they learn
something well, it tends to be well retained, particularly if it is
periodically reviewed and tested. It is also known, however, that
pupils vary a great deal in the rate at which they learn - some
learn very fast, others much slower, but, despite these differences
in rate of learning, nearly all pupils can learn what they are sup-
posed to learn in school, given enough time. The author believes
that teaching ought to be a simple matter if it is viewed as a process concerned with the management of learning. He believes that
the function of the teacher is to specify what is to be learned, to

* Carroll, John B. "Problems of Measurement Related to the Concept of Learning for Mastery," Educational Horizons, 48, No. 3
(1970), 71-80. Reprinted with the permission of the publisher,
Mr. Frederick Tyler, and the author.

motivate pupils to learn it, to provide them with instructional
materials, to administer these learning materials at a rate suitable for each pupil, to monitor students' progress, to diagnose
difficulties and provide proper remediation for them, to give
praise and encouragement for good performance, and to give review and practice that will maintain pupils' learnings over long
periods of time. Is this a simple matter? Yes, if the teacher
knows his trade.

But what goes on in the schools all too often belies these
statements. Teachers do not clearly outline what is to be learned;
they fail to motivate students; they ignore individual differences in
pupils' rate of learning and capacity to absorb skills and knowledge; they fail to monitor students' progress adequately; they are
unable adequately to diagnose pupils' learning difficulties or to
remedy them; they fail to give feedback on pupils' progress or to
use techniques of praise and reward effectively; they fail to attend
to maintaining pupils' learnings over long periods of time.

The author has tried to look at school learning from the
standpoint of an experimental psychologist of learning, and he does
not think this is entirely impractical. When a psychologist takes
a somewhat backward child out of a schoolroom to administer an
experimental learning situation, he finds that when he properly
controls the learning situation, the child does learn and retain
what he learns. It is not simply the novelty of the situation that
makes the difference; it is something about the way the experimental psychologist manages the learning situation in a way different from what goes on in the classroom.

With some of the well-established principles of educational
psychology in mind, a "model of school learning" was formulated
by the author that contains the basic features of learning and allows
one to analyze good and bad teaching situations (Carroll, 1963).
Presented first in 1963, in the Teachers College Record, this
"model of school learning" later inspired Benjamin Bloom of the
University of Chicago to derive a concept of "mastery learning"
that, if properly applied, should make it possible for all or nearly
all pupils to attain the basic skills and knowledges that are the
essential goals of every school curriculum.

Before getting into the technical details of measurement problems allied with mastery learning, it might be well to review
briefly the features of the model of school learning and the way in
which it can lead to Bloom's "mastery learning."

The model of school learning is oriented around the analysis
of what may be called "learning tasks." A learning task may be of
any size or complexity. It may be the learning of a single association or concept; it may be the learning of the materials in a particular two-week unit of a course; it may be the learning of the

material in a total course or even a four-year curriculum. Obviously, it is often important to analyze the more complex tasks into subtasks. It is most essential, however, to be able to state as exactly as possible what the learning task is, particularly its objectives, in testable form. That is, a teacher must be able to determine when a student has mastered the task to a satisfactory degree. Learning psychologists speak of this matter in terms of setting a criterion for satisfactory performance. Recently, there has been much emphasis on trying to specify criteria in "behavioral" terms, and the author believes this is a desirable emphasis even if it is not always possible to make such specifications.

Now, suppose that the teacher is considering a particular learning task, and suppose also that he has optimal means of teaching this task to students. Suppose also that the students are willing to work at this learning until they reach the stated criterion, and that the teacher provides opportunity for them to do so. Even under these conditions, there will be great variation in the amount of time taken by different students to learn the task.

A number of research studies suggest that the bottom 5 percent of the students will take about five times as long as the top 5 percent of the students. The time that a given student will take may be thought of as a time-line:

      start   criterion
                                                attainment

                 ← time →

The line for the faster student will, of course, be short, while it may be very long for the slower student. In fact, it is necessary to allow for the possibility that some students will never reach criterion; for such students, one may think of the length of the line as infinite. When the task is very difficult, or when it depends upon very special aptitudes, there may be quite a number of students who will never "make it." After all, not very many runners can make a mile in four minutes, and not every piano student can become a concert artist. But for most of the tasks in the regular school curriculum, it can be expected that every student will reach criterion if given enough time - a time within reason. This is one of the optimistic aspects of the model of school learning.

The amount of time that a student needs to learn a given task under optimal learning conditions is, in the author's opinion, a reflection of some basic characteristic or characteristics of the student that may be called "aptitude." Why pupils vary in the amount of time they need for a given learning task is not known; variations in aptitude are, in the author's opinion, simply a given

for the educator to deal with in the best possible way. Often one
can use various tests and other indicators to predict learning time,
and the use of aptitude predictors will sometimes help in dealing
with variations in learning time. Learning time for a given task
is often a complex function of a number of basic aptitudes - verbal
ability, memory ability, spatial ability, and so forth, as they have
been identified by factor analysis studies, or more recently in
J. P. Guilford's (1967) work on the "structure of intellect."
        Much is said about student motivation. There can be various
sources of motivation but, from the author's point of view, the
basic fact is that students vary in the amount of time they are willing to spend on learning. No matter what their interest is, or how
they are motivated, if they spend the amount of time they need on
learning the task, they will learn to criterion. There is, in fact,
a good deal of research evidence that suggests that student interest
is not correlated with success in learning. But this is not to say
that the teacher should not be concerned with motivation; it is the
teacher's task to manage the child's learning so that he will spend
the requisite amount of time, and anything that the teacher or
curriculum designer can do to enhance the child's motivation and
interest will be all to the good. But in analyzing a given learning
situation, teachers do have to consider how much time a given
pupil is willing to spend on it if left to his own devices. Suppose,
for example, one has a pupil who for one reason or another is not
willing to spend the amount of time he needs; he spends only m
amount of time. This situation can be represented by putting a
mark on the pupil's aptitude time-line, thus:

start   criterion
                              m   attainment

Obviously, if the child is not motivated to spend more time, his
learning will be incomplete; he will not attain mastery.
        But there is another time variable that is extremely important
in analyzing school practices; this is the variable that the author
calls opportunity to learn. Often the school curriculum and schedule
is organized in such a way that many students do not have enough
time to learn. In group instruction, a teacher must give, for
example, two weeks for the learning of a unit, ignoring or laying
aside the fact that some students could learn it in a much shorter
time, and that other students would require a much longer time.
The essential virtue of what is called "individualized instruction"
is that it allows each student to learn at his own rate - not necessarily an "ad libitum" rate completely under the control of the
student, but one that is necessary and efficient for him. This
"opportunity to learn" variable can be represented by another

mark on the student's aptitude time-line:

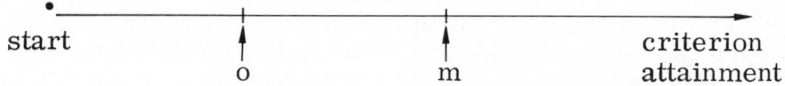

start   criterion
                  o   m   attainment

In this illustration the author has placed the "opportunity to learn"
mark in such a way as to show a case where a student is not even
given as much time to learn as he is willing to spend, even though
the amount of time he is willing to spend is still short of the amount
of time he really needs. Obviously this student is going to fall far
short of completely mastering the learning task.

    The model of school learning includes two other variables
that cannot be directly represented in terms of time, but the author
assumes that they affect the amount of time a student needs and,
therefore, the degree of mastery that he will attain. These two
variables are: (1) the quality of instruction and (2) the student's
ability to understand and profit from instruction. The author assumes that these variables interact, and, indeed, there is considerable research evidence that they can and do. For example, students who have a high ability to understand and profit from instruction are little affected by variations in quality of instruction, while
students with low ability to understand instruction are much more
affected by variations in quality. Ability to understand and profit
from instruction is probably associated with verbal intelligence
and reasoning ability. Thus, students with high verbal intelligence
can learn pretty well even with a poor program of instruction.

    With reference to the student's aptitude time-line, the effect
of poor quality of instruction interacting with poor ability to understand instruction is to increase the required learning time beyond
what would be required under optimal conditions:

start   (normal time   (criterion
                         for criterion   attainment
                         attainment)   under poor
                                                   instruction)

Thus, poor quality of instruction tends, particularly for the less
verbally able students, to decrease the student's chances of attaining complete mastery, because the extra time that would be required is often beyond what the schedule can allow. There are
many aspects of "quality of instruction," but the author would
emphasize those that have to do with sequencing the order of presentation of material from simple to more complex, with making
sure that each stage is properly mastered before the next one is
taken up, and with making sure that the pupil understands exactly
what the objectives of instruction are. The quality of the instruc-

tional materials, and the teacher's grasp of the subject matter
and ability to diagnose children's difficulties are important factors
in quality of instruction, but the major factors center in what may
be called the teacher's ability to "manage" the course of learning.

Doubtless there are still more interactions among the components of this model. For example, good quality of instruction tends
to enhance students' interest and willingness to spend the required
amount of time on learning. Properly controlled individualized
instruction can also enhance motivation; for the bright, apt student
it keeps him working on tasks that continually interest and challenge
him, and for the less apt student it enhances self-esteem and confidence by giving him experiences of success rather than failure.

The importance of prior learnings should also be mentioned.
In the figures presented here, the author has assumed that the student is "starting from scratch" in whatever learning task he is un-
dertaking. But new learning tasks are often taken up in the usual
school situation without regard for the fact that some students are
already well along in achieving the objectives of the task. Some
may even have already learned whatever is being taught. It is
inefficient and stultifying to treat them as if they were beginners.
Where possible, it would be desirable to place them far enough
along in the learning sequence to give them a challenge without its
being utterly frustrating.

In this discussion, the author has been attempting to make
the point that "mastery learning" can be attained through control
of the various factors in the learning process so that all students,
or as many students as possible, will achieve the desired objectives
of instruction. The goal is for every student to get to the end of
his aptitude time-line, and to do so as quickly as possible, even
though it is recognized that it will take different pupils different
amounts of time.

In a way, there is nothing new in what has been said here.
Individualized instruction by private tutors was practiced even by
the Greeks and Romans of classical times. In the present century,
the Winnetka plan introduced in the 1920's by Carleton Washburne
(1922) and his associates was an attempt to take account of individual differences in required learning times. If it was not a complete
success (and it wasn't), it was probably because an adequate
technology of instruction was not yet available. The technological
innovations of the last decade, however, have permitted more
flexible arrangements; for example, the experiment in Individually
Prescribed Instruction introduced by Robert Glaser at the Pittsburgh Learning Research and Development Center, and the work
in computer-assisted instruction introduced by Patrick Suppes and
Richard Atkinson at Stanford University. But there are many other
instances, not all well publicized, where individualized instruction

has been made successful, not necessarily with elaborate technological gadgetry. Much can be done with fairly simple equipment
and materials.

The author's intention has been to review the model of school
learning and the concept of mastery learning in order to get around
to discussing problems of measurement. The better the various
components of the learning model can be measured, the better it
will be possible to manage learning to produce mastery.

MEASURING THE CRITERION ACHIEVEMENT

First, the problem of the criterion might be considered, that
is, determining whether a student has, in fact, achieved the goals
of a learning task. This has always been a standard problem in
measurement, and, in view of the extensive literature on the subject,
it is not necessary to dwell on it. There are many ways of going
about assessing the results of learning - - standardized tests, specific criterion tests, performance tests, transfer tests, teacher
interviews and observations, and so forth.

Standardized tests are, if anything, used too much, and too
much reliance is placed on their results. The main problem with
a standardized test is that it is likely not to be exactly appropriate
to the learning task as it is defined in a particular curriculum.
The standardized test of reading comprehension may give the student a series of tasks in reading that fail to measure the precise
skills the teacher has sought to teach, because the construction
and standardization of the test has been aimed at a more general
"common denominator" kind of curriculum. Furthermore, the
overall score or grade level index yielded by the standardized test
does not usually provide adequate information about which skills
and knowledges have been well acquired by a particular student,
and which skills he has failed to acquire. A sixth-grade pupil
might get a sixth-grade reading level by virtue of a good recognition vocabulary, despite having poor overall comprehension of
sentence and paragraph structure. Frederick B. Davis (1968) has
demonstrated that reading comprehension tests measure a fairly
mixed bag of language comprehension skills.

Yet, the construction of tests that are specifically aimed at
the goals of a particular learning task has its difficulties. For one
thing, many learning tasks are extremely complex. Adequate
reading comprehension, for example, can depend upon knowledge
of the meanings of thousands of words; it is impossible to sample
them all. In assessing competence in a foreign language, one does
not know how to sample the range of vocabulary and grammar that
constitutes competence; some would say that it is impossible to do

so because the vocabulary and grammar of a language cannot be
completely described. The author does not necessarily agree
with this counsel of despair, but, even so, it has been found that
"global" tests of communicative competence in a foreign language
are perhaps more valid in terms of curricular objectives than tests
using the "discrete point" approach in which knowledges of language
facts are tested one by one. For another thing,practical consider-
ations often dictate testing competences that are only indirectly
related to the true goals of teaching. Testing spelling by having
students recognize misspellings is not necessarily highly correlated with spelling skill in free composition. The author can suggest
here only a few of the many problems that come up in criterion-
performance evaluation. Yet, he believes that most educational
researchers would agree that "criterion-referenced" tests are
best for determining whether a pupil has reached the goals of a
learning task. "Criterion-referenced tests" are, of course, the
kinds of tests whose results indicate as precisely as possible
whether the pupil has achieved the goals specified for the learning
task, rather than merely placing the pupil on some sort of relative
scale of goodness. The construction of such tests demands much
skill and insight, and it is probably a task that requires special
attention and expertise, wherever it can be found in a school system.

     Michael Scriven (1967) has made the useful distinction between
"formative" evaluation and "summative" evaluation. Achievement
tests given at the end of major units or periods of instruction are
likely to fall into the category of "summative" tests for they attempt
to "sum up" total achievement in a course. This is where problems
of sampling from course content become acute. "Formative"
evaluation, on the other hand, refers to tests and other evaluations
applied in the course of learning - - the sooner the better. Formative tests can have two purposes: (1) to find out how much pupils
have learned in a restricted area of content, for example, at the
end of a unit of instruction and (2) to assess whether instruction
has been properly designed and conducted. It is much easier to
construct and use formative tests - - often they can be constructed
by the teacher at appropriate intervals during a course, rather
than at the end, when there is little time to remedy any deficiencies
disclosed by the tests. And, in any case, tests or other indicants
of learning should be taken at short intervals through a course of
instruction for diagnostic and remedial purposes. They serve
one of the main functions of managing learning, namely, to track
students' progress in the course of instruction and provide appropriate feedback of information to the student, whether it be praise for
solid accomplishment or cues to where the student is having difficulty. It is less important to give "grades" or marks to the student
than to give him clear information as to what he has learned and

what he still needs to learn. In fact, many people have recommended that no grades at all be assigned on the basis of "formative"
tests, since they are simply a means of quality control on the output of learning. Better still, build the testing function into the
instruction itself, as is often done in so-called "programmed
instruction. "

Recently, the author saw, at the Hawaii Curriculum Center,
in an experimental school project directed by Gerald Dykstra, an
interesting new wrinkle in pupil evaluation. Part of the evaluation
process and indeed of the learning process, even in the first and
second grades, was to permit a pupil to go ahead to another unit
of learning only after he himself had not only passed a test on it
but had also "taught" the material to another pupil, or at least
given another pupil a simple test of learning. Most of the "testing"
was, in fact, done by the pupils themselves; simple testing tools
were used for this purpose, for example, a series of flashcards
set up on a little board so that they could be turned over one by
one, something like the leaves of a desk calendar. The teacher's
main function, in this case, was to supervise the whole show,
directing each child to his individual learning or testing task. The
children seemed to enjoy this kind of arrangement, and impressive
charts showed their progress.

RATE OF LEARNING
_____

Now what about "rate of learning ?" How can it be measured ?
What is the course of learning ? Because pupils do vary so much
in their rates of learning, there has been much interest in measuring rate and, if possible, controlling it, within the context of the
author's model of school learning and the associated concept of
mastery learning. Suppes (1964), in his article on children's
learning of mathematics, pointed out that rates vary enormously
even when instruction seems to be near optimal. And C. Mauritz
Lindvall, John Bolvin, and Margaret Wang, at the Pittsburgh
Learning Research and Development Center, have made detailed
studies of these rate variations. They have investigated different
methods of measuring rate, with the somewhat puzzling result
that different measures of rate are not necessarily highly correlated. Further, they find that rate of learning is by no means
constant over various learning tasks. In part, the author would
have predicted such a result, because it is his assumption that
rate of learning may be quite specific to a given task, dependent
as it is on specific aptitudes and prior learnings. Perhaps, too,
rate of learning depends partly on a inherent human variability in
performance level. Everyone has the experience of rapid

accomplishment on some days and sluggishness on other days,
dependent on physiological state, the weather, personal relations,
or whatever. On the other hand, over long periods of time and
over many different kinds of tasks, rate of learning does seem to
have an underlying constancy.

Fundamentally, rate of learning should be measured in terms
of amount of skill or knowledge gained per unit of time. But the
nature of the learning task will partly determine the shape of the
learning curve - - which is, after all, a reflection of learning rate.
Some tasks are of such a nature that amount of gain is approximately linear per unit of time; this is true when the learning task
itself consists of a large number of subtasks, each learnable in
approximately the same amount of time. The author finds this to
be true, for example, of foreign language learning, where the
increments of new vocabulary and grammar points are approximately constant from lesson to lesson. Under conditions where
the learner can proceed at his own rate, as in programmed instruction, the variations in rate reflect the fact that people take
different amounts of time to learn the same amount. For example,
in an experiment in programmed instruction in Chinese, the author
(1963) found that rates varied from 15 frames per hour to 50
frames per hour, and these rates held up remarkably well over
many hours of instruction, up to 35 hours in some cases. (The
"frames" were longer and richer in content than the usual small-
step frames, and, furthermore, students had to repeat sequences
of frames until they mastered them; the rates which have been
given are based on net progress through the program.) It was
rather striking to see some people apparently taking in the material
quite rapidly, others sitting gazing at the material for minutes at
a time.

Other learning tasks may show the typical negatively accelerated learning curve, for example, learning a list of new words to
be spelled, and still others may show the kind of learning curve
associated with "insightful" learning, that is, where there is no
appreciable progress for a considerable period of time, with a
sudden spurt of performance as the learner achieves understanding
or skill. The author believes, therefore, that the nature of the
learning task must be taken into account in measuring learning
rate, and also in measuring degree of learning. In his original
statement of the model, he asserted only that the degree of
learning is some function of the ratio:

$$\frac{\text{Time taken to learn}}{\text{Time needed to learn}}$$

If the amount learned is a linear function of time, the degree of
learning (in terms of a proportion) is a direct, linear function of

this ratio. But if the amount learned is not a linear function of
time, degree of learning is also not a linear function of the ratio.
Douglas D. Sjogren (1967) studied a case in which he concluded
that degree of learning is an approximately linear function of the
ratio (time taken)/(time needed), but it should be noted that this
is only one case out of many possible ones. Only by study of a
variety of situations would it be possible to make any generaliza-
tions about the constancy of rate of learning over time. All this
assumes, of course, that it is possible to measure amounts of
gain in equal units - - an assumption that is usually very shaky.

In practice, it is useful to plot student progress over time.
Even if the units by which "amount of learning" is measured are
not equal, the teacher can watch progress, just as a physician
watches a temperature or weight chart. Publishers of standardized
tests should provide charts on which pupil progress can be plotted,
in addition to the "profiles" they frequently provide. If they are
not provided by the publisher, the teacher can easily make these
graphs on ordinary squared paper.

In the model of school learning, the true amount of time that
a student needs to learn something is a variable that unfortunately
cannot be observed directly since it assumes that the student is
well-motivated (that is, he is willing to spend all necessary time
to learn), and that instruction is optimal. The total time to reach
criterion is, of course, directly observable, but only for students
who reach criterion, and even then, failure of instruction to be
optimal may make that time longer than would be necessary. The
author frankly does not know how to measure the true value of
"time needed to learn" by any given student; perhaps one could
solve for this value if we had a complete network of equations con-
necting the various components of the model and also could get
accurate estimates of the other parameters. But such a network
of equations is far in the future and would not ordinarily be practical for school use unless one had a computer.

Nevertheless, there are several ways in which time needed
to learn can be estimated. If there is reason to believe that
amount learned is a linear function of time, total time needed to
reach criterion might be predicted by projecting from early stages
of learning. For example, if one had a program of instruction that
contained 1,000 units or "frames" - - not really a large number - -
and a student took 10 hours to master the first 100, it is a reasonable guess that he would take 100 hours to do the whole lot. But if
it were known that amount learned is a negatively accelerated function of time, such that the student would slow down in later stages
of learning, the estimate of time needed might be considerably
longer.

The best way of estimating time needed is to use tests of

relevant aptitudes and prior learnings. It happens, in fact, that
the author originally developed the model of school learning in the
context of his work on the prediction of success in foreign languages.
He found that a battery that he developed, now called the Modern
Language Aptitude Test, was an excellent predictor of rate of
learning foreign languages, particularly when the student had no
prior training in the language. The test was used extensively by
the Foreign Service Institute of the U. S. Department of State in
selecting candidates for language training. As experience was
developed with the test, it became possible to state approximately
how much training time would be needed by a person with a given
level of foreign language aptitude to get to a given level of profi-
ciency in a given foreign language. Since foreign languages vary
in difficulty, different values had to be predicted for "easy" languages like Italian and Dutch and for "hard" languages like Arabic
and Vietnamese.

It can be seen from this example that a considerable amount
of research is necessary to develop prediction tables. The author
does not know any instance in which a similar amount of research
has been done to develop prediction tables for time needed to learn
school subjects. But such research would be possible. As matters
stand, there is considerable information available about the validi-
ties of certain tests in predicting progress in reading, elementary
school mathematics, and other subjects. Progress, however, has
been measured in terms of amount learned in a constant amount of
time, and it would be difficult to connect these results with estimates of total time needed, because these tests have rarely been
used in the context of individualized instruction and research
thereon.

But there is a complicating factor in all this. There is some
evidence that aptitude interacts, in many school learning situations,
with the kind of instruction offered. If this is so, quality of instruction is partly a matter of whether instruction is properly adapted
to students' aptitudes. Lee J. Cronbach and Richard E. Snow
(1969) completed a comprehensive review of the aptitude-treatment
interaction literature and concluded that while few definite interactions of this type have been confirmed, this was a research area
worth exploring. Several recent doctoral dissertations appear to
have found significant interactions. For example, John B. Davis
(1967) found that certain of Guilford's "structure of intellect" factors interacted with type of instruction in mathematics such that
students with good abilities in "cognition of semantic classes"
were much better off when they were taught with "semantic methods"
as opposed to "symbolic" methods. Conversely, students with
good "symbolic" abilities were much better off under instruction
that stressed symbolic content. Rates of learning, therefore,

may vary not only with different aptitudes but also with different
methods of instruction. Unfortunately this is a rather new field
of research, and very little can be said about it right now that
would be of practical use to the schoolman or teacher.

Amount of time needed to learn is obviously a function of
how much has been learned already. Here again there are important problems of measurement. If one can measure what the child
already knows, he may be able to save the time of both teacher
and child. Various programs of instruction are now coming out
with built-in tests to determine where to place the student in the
learning sequence. Of necessity, these tests try to get at the
specifics of learning, for example to find out what letters of the
alphabet the child knows when he starts to read. Actually, for
many of these learning situations, the best judge of amount of
prior learning and readiness may be the teacher.

There is a converse case, namely where a particular program
of instruction assumes certain prior learnings, but where the student actually does not have these prior learnings. For example, in
teaching statistics at the graduate level the author wanted to be
able to assume that the student already knew how to handle simple
algebraic expressions; all too often, however, he found through
tests that the student had never acquired these skills or had forgotten them through disuse. Remedial work was, therefore, necessary in order to prepare students for the course.

Some educational psychologists have postulated that aptitude
tests are essentially achievement tests that measure the presence
or absence of prior learnings or, as they are sometimes called,
"entry behaviors." If this is the case, they reason, it should be
possible to train students in these entry behaviors. Very little is
known about whether this is actually possible. The author can say
that in the case of foreign language aptitude, efforts to "train"
aptitudes have been highly unsuccessful. In fact, one project of
this type, conducted by Robert Politzer at Stanford University,
nearly caused a rebellion among the students of the project. It
was found that it not only seemed impossible to improve the aptitudes of low-aptitude students but that the students also complained
about the apparent irrelevance of the aptitude training to learning
foreign languages. On the basis of experiences like this, the
author believes that it is best to use aptitude tests simply to predict rate of learning, without trying to "improve" the aptitudes
that are measured by such tests. Apparently some aptitudes are
more or less impervious to training. But this may not be true of
all aptitudes, some of which may be reflections of deficient "entry
behaviors" or prior learnings.

MEASURING ABILITY TO UNDERSTAND INSTRUCTION

The author thinks of this as a very general aptitude that
applies to all academic subjects and even possibly to some subjects
that may be only marginally academic such as music or physical
education. Since most instruction is conveyed by verbal means,
often using a quite broad range of language elements, the student
must be able to understand this verbal instruction. Tests of verbal
intelligence are, therefore, the methods of choice, but probably
some emphasis should be given to the measurement of listening
comprehension. Sam Duker's bibliography of research on listening
(1968) contains many reports of research showing that listening
comprehension tests can predict school success.

As previously stated, ability to understand instruction interacts with quality of instruction. One means of improving instruction is to make it more easily comprehensible. The vocabulary
and conceptual load of instructional materials can be adjusted to
this end. There is now a large literature on the measurement of
the reading difficulty or "readability" of written materials (see
George R. Klare, 1963 and John R. Bormuth, 1968). Sometimes
written materials are quite unnecessarily complex. For example,
Edmund B. Coleman (1964) has shown that someone may write a
sentence such as the following:

"Our goal is the achievement of the highest good for
society, to be attained through a correct definition of
names."

This sentence might, however, be much more easily understood if
all nominalizations were changed to active verbs, as follows:

"Our goal is that we achieve the highest good for
society, and we can attain this when we define names
correctly."

MEASURING QUALITY OF INSTRUCTION

Probably the most difficult measurement task connected with
the model of school learning is the measurement of the quality of
instruction.

Ideally, one might think that the most valid measure of instruction is to measure average pupil gain under different teachers or
different instructional systems. Teachers do vary enormously in
their ability to teach. Some years ago, for example, the author
found that the reading achievement of pupils in the third grade was

much better predicted by knowing what teacher they had in the
second grade than by knowing what teacher they had in the third
grade: apparently some second grade teachers were highly successful in teaching reading, while others were far from successful. N. L. Gage, at Stanford, has established that teachers differ
reliably in their ability to "put across" a lesson in lecture form.
In practice, however, it is difficult to measure quality of instruction by comparisons between teachers unless a multitude of other
factors can be ruled out.

Incidentally, the author believes that the attempt to measure
teacher effectiveness by check lists and observational schedules
such as those proposed by some educational researchers is likely
to be only minimally successful, mainly because the ability of the
teacher to manage instruction is more a matter of how he or she
applies proper controls over a long period of time. Thus, observation of a teacher during a short period, such as one class hour,
or even on several separate occasions, is unlikely to yield information on how well the teacher observes and monitors the long-term
progress of individual students or provides proper feedback and
remediation. Some other ways to get this type of information
should be explored.

One promising technique was discovered a number of years
ago by one of the author's students, Morris L. Cogan (1958), but
apparently this discovery never has been followed up. He found
that the students themselves were able to make very revealing
appraisals of their teachers when they were asked to state how
much voluntary "extra work" their teachers inspired them to do.
This was, at least, a way of getting at the motivating function of
teachers.

Some evidence compels me to believe that one important
aspect of the quality of instruction is the extent to which the
teacher makes plain exactly what the learning task is, setting
forth the objectives in a way that the student knows what he has to
learn and accomplish in order to achieve those goals. (This
aspect of quality of instruction may reside in the instructional
materials as well as in the teacher.) There is a need for a way to
measure how well the teacher or the instructional materials give
assignments and specify learning objectives.

Another aspect of the quality of instruction has to do with how
well materials are sequenced and graded. Robert M. Gagné and
Noel E. Paradise (1961) were pioneers in showing that learning
subtasks can often be arranged in a hierarchy such that mastery of
the easier tasks is necessary,but not sufficient,for the mastery of
the more difficult or complex tasks. Showing that learning subtasks
form such a hierarchy requires rather special techniques of statistical analysis. Student performance on each pair of tasks has to

be examined for a particular pattern of scores, whereby all who
pass the harder task must also pass the easier task, and none who
fail the easier task succeed on the harder task. Recent research
has gone in the direction of trying to discover such hierarchies of
learning tasks and their properties and to determine whether pupils
learn better when the tasks are properly sequenced in instruction.
If so, this will be one useful indicator of quality of instruction.

Finally, the author has already mentioned the important role
of "formative" or diagnostic tests, plus the feedback from such
tests, in contributing to the quality of instruction. The teacher
who makes judicious use of such tests and is able to provide encouragement and praise, or corrective feedback, as the case may
be, is probably a more effective teacher than one who makes only
casual or insignificant use of such tests. This is another example
of a teacher behavior that is unlikely to be properly or reliably
observed in the time-sampling, checklist type of teacher behavior
research.

MEASURING "PERSEVERANCE"

Perseverance, or one might call it "stick-to-itiveness", is
probably the most difficult component of all to measure or to predict. In theory, it is a function of the time the student is willing
to spend on active learning, not just passive reception or the kind
of daydreaming that all too often occurs while the student seems to
be studying or learning. One proposal is to measure how much
time the student is willing to spend by observing how much time he
does spend. Margaret Wang at the Pittsburgh Learning Research
and Development Center tried to do this, observing a time sample
of each student's behavior while he was working on a unit of study
and determining the percent of time that he appeared overtly atten-
tive to his lesson materials. Unfortunately these measures showed
little correlation, if any, with any measure of student progress.
But perhaps measures of time spent in homework or in language
laboratories, where the student may have considerable freedom in
planning his schedule, will show some relationships with progress.
George R. Thornton (1939) found that there is indeed a general
trait of persistence or perseverance, and some of the tests that he
devised might be adaptable for school use.

Probably it is not too important to measure or predict perseverance; it is more important to enhance it. There is abundant
evidence to suggest that perseverance is largely a function of prior
experiences of success or failure with similar learning tasks.
Often these experiences of success and failure go back to the earliest school years; it must be in these years that it is particularly

important to arrange instruction so as to yield experiences of success for all children irrespective of ability. But the basic principles apply at any age, and recent research evidence comes out loud and clear for the desirability of administering learning tasks in such a way that all learners will experience much more success than failure. Small failures can perhaps be instructive, but large, enduring failures lead only to frustration and withdrawal from learning. One does not have to be a rabid "reinforcement theorist" to accept this fact. In fact, success experiences during learning tend to create interest in learning even when none existed before.

This article has tried to identify and explain the major measurement problems associated with the model of school learning. Much of what has been said, unfortunately, lies in the realm of future research. It is the author's hope that an understanding of the basic concepts and principles on the part of teachers and school administrators will yield helpful suggestions in the direction of improving school learning.

REFERENCES

Bormuth, John R. (ed.). Readability in 1968. National Conference on Research in English, National Council of Teachers of English, 1968.

Carroll, John B. "A Model of School Learning," Teachers College Record, 64 (1963), 723-33.

Carroll, John B. Programmed Self-Instruction in Mandarin Chinese: Observations of Student Progress with an Automated Audiovisual Instructional Device. Wellesley, Massachusetts: Language Testing Fund, 1963. (Available from ERIC Document Reproduction Service, Document No. ED 022-374.)

Cogan, Morris L. "The Behavior of Teachers and the Productive Behavior of Their Pupils: I. Perception Analysis, II. Trait Analysis," Journal of Experimental Education, 27 (1958), 89-124.

Coleman, Edmund B. "The Comprehensibility of Several Grammatical Transformations," Journal of Applied Psychology, 48, no. 3 (1964), 186-90.

Cronbach, Lee J. and Richard E. Snow. Individual Differences in Learning Ability as a Function of Instructional Variables. Final Report. USOE, Contract No. OEC 4-6-061269-1217.

Stanford, California: Stanford University, School of Education, 1969.

Davis, Frederick B. "Research in Comprehension in Reading," Reading Research Quarterly, 3, no. 4 (1968), 499-545.

Davis, John B, Jr. "An Investigation of the Interaction of Certain Instructional Strategies with the Structure of Basic Mental Abilities in the Learning of Some Mathematical Operations." Unpublished Ph.D. dissertation, Florida State University, 1967.

Duker, Sam. Listening Bibliography. Second Edition. Metuchen, New Jersey: Scarecrow Press, 1968.

Gagne, Robert M. and Noel E. Paradise. "Abilities and Learning Sets in Knowledge Acquisition," Psychological Monographs, 75, no. 14 (1961).

Guilford, J. P. The Nature of Human Intelligence. New York: McGraw-Hill Book Co., Inc., 1967.

Klare, George R. The Measurement of Readability. Ames, Iowa: Iowa State University Press, 1963.

Scriven, Michael. "The Methodology of Evaluation," in Ralph W. Tyler, et al., Perspectives of Curriculum Evaluation. Chicago: Rand McNally, 1967. (AERA Monograph Series on Curriculum Evaluation, I) pp. 39-83.

Sjogren, Douglas D. "Achievement as a Function of Study Time," American Educational Research Journal, 4 (1967), 337-43.

Suppes, Patrick. "Modern Learning Theory and the Elementary School Curriculum," American Educational Research Journal, 4 (1964), 79-93.

Thornton, George R. "A Factor Analysis of Tests Designed To Measure Persistence," Psychological Monographs, 51, no. 229 (1939).

Washburne, Carleton W. "Educational Measurements as a Key to Individualizing Instruction and Promotion," Journal of Educational Research, 5 (1922), 195-206.

Chapter 4

MASTERY LEARNING*

Benjamin S. Bloom, University of Chicago

The most wasteful and destructive aspect of our present educational system is the set of expectations about student learning each teacher brings to the beginning of a new course or term. The instructor expects a third of his pupils to learn well what is taught, a third to learn less well, and a third to fail or just "get by." These expectations are transmitted to the pupils through school grading policies and practices and through the methods and materials of instruction. Students quickly learn to act in accordance with them, and the final sorting through the grading process approximates the teacher's original expectations. A pernicious self-fulfilling prophecy has been created.

Such a system fixes the academic goals of teachers and students. It reduces teachers' aspirations and students' desire for further learning. Further, it systematically destroys the ego and self-concept of a sizeable proportion of students who are legally required to attend school for ten to twelve years under conditions which are repeatedly frustrating and humiliating. The costs of such a system in reducing student opportunities for further learning

* Adapted from "Learning for Mastery," U. C. L. A. - C. S. E. I. P. Evaluation Comment, 1, no. 2 (1968). Printed with the permission of the author.

and in alienating youth from both school and society are too great
to be borne for long.

Most student (perhaps over 90 per cent) <u>can</u> master what we
teach. Our basic instructional task is to define what we mean by
mastery of a subject and to discover methods and materials to
help the largest proportion of our students reach it.

BACKGROUND

Underdeveloped or undeveloped societies can utilize only a
small number of highly educated persons in the economy and can
afford to assist only a few students to complete secondary or higher
education. In such societies, much of the task of the schools and
the external examining system is to select the talented few who are
to be given advanced educational opportunities and to reject the
majority of students at various points in the educational process.
Such societies invest more in the prediction and selection of talent
than in its development.

The complexity of the skills required by the work force of any
highly developed nation like the United States, however, suggests
we can no longer assume that completion of secondary and advanced
education is for the few. Investment in human resources through
education has a greater return rate than capital investment (Schultz,
1963; Bowman, 1966). We cannot return to an economy in which
educational opportunities are scarce, but rather must provide enough
opportunities that the largest possible proportion of students will
acquire the skills and knowledge necessary to sustain the society's
growth.

In addition to concern for the society, we must also express
deep concern for the intellectual and personality consequences resulting from the lack of clear success in school learning experiences.
It reduces the students' desire for further learning. Increasingly,
however, learning throughout life (continued learning) will be
necessary for the largest proportion of the work force. School
learning must be successful and rewarding so that learning can
continue throughout the individual's life as needed. Even more
important, unsuccessful school learning experiences limit the areas
available in which the individual can search for values. As the
society has become more and more secular, personal values have
been restricted to the areas of hedonism, interpersonal relations,
self-development, and ideas. If the schools frustrate students in
the latter two areas, only the first two are left open for further
exploration. Whatever the case may be for each of these value
areas, the schools must strive to give all students successful learning experiences in the realms of ideas and self-development.

Unquestionably, schools now provide perhaps one-third of all students with successful learning experiences. However, if they are to provide successful learning experiences for at least 90 per cent, then major changes must take place in the policies, practices, and attitudes of teachers and administrators and in the attitudes of students.

THE NORMAL CURVE

The normal grading curve has been used so long that educators have come to believe in it. Achievement measures are designed to detect even trivial differences among learners so that we may then assign grades in a normal fashion. We expect about 10 per cent to receive A's and are quite prepared to fail an equal proportion. Students' failure is frequently determined by their ranked position within the class rather than their inability to grasp the central ideas of the subject matter. It does not matter that the students failed one year performed as well as the C students of another, nor that they performed as well as the A students in another school.

Having become "conditioned" to the normal distribution, we set grading policies in these terms and are horrified if a teacher recommends a new grading distribution. Administrators are constantly on the alert to control teachers who grade "too easy" or "too hard" while teachers who use the normal curve escape difficulty. Even more alarming, we convince students that they can only do C or D work through the grading system and through quizzes and progress testing. Finally, we teach as though only a minority of our students are able to learn.

The normal curve is not sacred. It describes the outcome of a random process. Since education is a purposeful activity in which we seek to have students learn what we teach, the achievement distribution should be very different from the normal curve if our instruction is effective. In fact, our educational efforts may be said to be unsuccessful to the extent that student achievement is normally distributed.

That "individual differences" between learners exist is indisputable. What is disputable is that these variations must play a role in student learning and must be reflected in our learning standards and achievement criteria. The fact that they do play a role in student learning and are reflected in the standards and criteria is due to our present policies and practices rather than to the necessities of the case. A fundamental task in education is to develop strategies which will take into account individual differences in such a way as to promote rather than inhibit the fullest development of the individual.

THE VARIABLES FOR MASTERY LEARNING STRATEGIES

One such strategy can be derived primarily from the work of Carroll (1963) supported by the ideas of Morrison (1926), Bruner (1966), Skinner (1954), Suppes (1966), Goodlad and Anderson (1959), and Glaser (1968). Although relevant research findings will be brought to bear throughout the presentation, our main concern is to focus on the major variables in a model of school learning and to suggest how these variables might be used in a strategy for mastery learning.

Briefly, the model proposed by Carroll (1963) indicates that if students are normally distributed with respect to aptitude for some subject and all students are given exactly the same instruction (in terms of amount and quality of instruction and learning time allowed), then achievement measured at the subject's completion will be normally distributed. Under such conditions the correlation between aptitude and achievement will be relatively high (r = +.70 or higher). Conversely, if students are normally distributed with respect to aptitude, but the kind and quality of instruction and learning time allowed are made appropriate to the characteristics and needs of each learner, the majority of students will achieve subject mastery. The correlation between aptitude and achievement should approach zero.

1. APTITUDE FOR PARTICULAR KINDS OF LEARNING

Individuals do differ in their aptitudes for particular kinds of learning, and over the years a large number of tests have been developed to measure these individual differences. These aptitude tests have proved relatively good predictors of achievement tests results and grades given by teachers. Consequently, their use has led many educators to believe that high achievement levels are possible only for students with high aptitudes and to infer a causal connection between aptitude and achievement. The simplest notion of causality is that students with high aptitude levels for a subject can learn its complex ideas while students with low aptitude levels can learn only its simplest.

In contrast is Carroll's (1963) view that aptitude is the amount of time required by the learner to attain mastery of a learning task. Implicit in this view is the assumption that given enough time, all students can conceivably attain mastery of any learning task. If Carroll is correct, then learning mastery is theoretically available to all if only we can find methods for helping each student. The available research supports Carroll's view. On both standardized tests and self-paced learning programs (Glaser, 1968; Atkinson, 1967), we find that most students attain a given criterion of achievement, but some will attain it much sooner than others.

Can all students learn a given task to the same high level of complexity? Studies of aptitude distributions in relation to student performance indicate that there are differences between the extreme (1 to 5 per cent at each end of the scale) students and the remainder of the population. At the top of the aptitude distribution there are likely to be some students who have a special talent for the subject. At the bottom, there are individuals with special disabilities for particular subjects. In between, however, are approximately 90 per cent of the students for whom we believe aptitudes are predictive of rate of learning rather than level or complexity of learning possible. Thus, we propose that 95 per cent of the students (the top 5 per cent plus the next 90 per cent) can learn a subject to a high level of mastery (for example, an A grade) if given sufficient learning time and appropriate types of help.

Some students will require more effort, time, and help to achieve this level. Therefore, a basic problem for a mastery learning strategy will be to find ways of reducing the learning time slower students require so that the task will not be prohibitively long and difficult for them.

We believe that aptitudes for particular learning tasks are not completely stable, and that they may be modified by appropriate environmental conditions or home and school learning experiences (Bloom, 1964; Hunt, 1961). It is likely that these aptitudes can be most markedly affected early in the child's home and school life. The central task of educational programs concerned with learning to learn and general education should be to produce positive changes in students' basic aptitudes. However, the key problem for strategies of mastery learning is to help students learn a subject to mastery whether or not changes are made in the aptitudes which are predictive of such learning.

2. QUALITY OF INSTRUCTION

Our schools have usually assumed that there should be a standard classroom situation for all students, typically consisting of group-based instruction with one teacher to about 30 students. All teachers are expected to teach a given subject in much the same way using the same text. Hence, over the years we have fallen into the "educational trap" of defining quality of instruction - - the effectiveness of teachers, teaching, instructional materials, curriculum - - in terms of group results. We persist in asking, "What is the best method of instruction for the group?", "Who is the best teacher for the group?", and "What is the best instructional material for the group?".

One may start, however, with the very different assumption that individual students may need very different types and qualities of instruction to learn the same content and instructional objectives to mastery levels. This is Carroll's view. He defines the quality of instruction in terms of the degree to which the presentation, explanation, and ordering of elements of the learning task approach the optimum for a given learner (Carroll, 1963).

Much research is needed to determine how learners' individual differences can be related to variations in the quality of instruction. The available research suggests that some students need more active involvement in the learning than others (Congreve, 1965). It also seems reasonable to expect that some students will need more concrete instructional cues, more practice, and more reinforcement than others.

We believe that if every student had a well-trained tutor, then most of them would be able to master a particular subject. The work of Dave (1963), for example, suggests that home tutoring is effectively used by middle-class parents when they believe that school instruction is not adaptive to their child's individual needs. Methods that can be used in the schools to obtain the same results must be found. The main point to be stressed is that quality of instruction must be developed with respect to the needs and characteristics of individual learners rather than groups of learners. Hopefully, future research will help determine the qualities and kinds of instruction needed by various types of learners.

3. ABILITY TO UNDERSTAND INSTRUCTION

The ability to understand instruction may be defined as the ability of the learner to understand the nature of the task he is to learn and the procedures he is to follow in its learning. In most high school and college courses, there is a single teacher and a single set of instructional materials. If the student can understand the teacher's communications and the instructional materials (usually a textbook), he will have little difficulty learning the subject. However, if he has difficulty understanding the teacher's instruction and/or the instructional materials, he will have great difficulty learning. Here is a major point at which the student's abilities interact with the instructional presentation and material. It is likely that in our highly verbal schools, a student's ability to understand instruction is determined largely by his verbal ability and reading comprehension. These two measures of language ability are highly correlated with achievement and grade point averages across subjects at the high school and college levels. This suggests that verbal ability (independent of specific subject aptitudes) determines some general ability to learn from teachers and instructional materials.

While it is possible to alter an individual's verbal ability, there are limits to the change that training can produce. Most change in verbal ability can be produced at the pre-school and elementary levels, with progressively less change likely as the student grows older (Bloom, 1964). The greatest immediate pay-off in dealing with the ability to understand instruction, therefore, is likely to result from modifications in the instruction to meet individual student needs. There is no doubt that some teachers already make these adjustments to fit the needs of a given group of students. Thus many teachers, often by habit or as a reflection of their attitudes, aim their instruction at the middle, top, or bottom group of students. There are, however, many instructional strategies which, given help and various types of aids, teachers can use to fit their instruction to the differing needs of all their students. Small-group study sessions consisting of two or three students are very effective in helping students overcome their learning difficulties in a cooperative rather than a competitive learning situation. Much depends upon the composition of the group and the opportunities each student is given to expose his learning problems and to have them corrected without demeaning himself and elevating another. Tutorial help is also extremely effective, though costly. Ideally, the tutor should be someone other than the teacher who brings a fresh point of view about a given idea and is capable of detecting student learning difficulties and fostering student self-reliance in learning.

Another approach to accommodating differences in students' ability to understand instruction is to vary the instructional materials. Alternative textbook explanations may prove effective at particular points in the instruction. Workbook and programed instruction units may be especially helpful for some students who need smaller steps, more drill, and frequent reinforcement. Others may learn a particular idea best through the concrete illustrations and high interest that audio-visual methods and academic games provide.

The important point is that the use of alternative methods of instruction and instructional materials is an attempt to improve the quality of instruction in relation to the ability of each student to understand that instruction. A particular student may use whatever variety of methods and materials found most useful as he encounters difficulties in his learning.

The presence and use of these alternative methods of instruction and instructional materials should help both teachers and

students overcome feelings of defeatism and passivity about learning. If a student can't learn in one way, he should be reassured
that alternatives are available to him; eventually, he should become able, independently, to identify the alternative methods and
materials he needs to complete his learning. The teacher should
come to recognize that it is student learning which is important
and that instructional alternatives exist by which he can help all
(or almost all) of his students learn his subject to a high level.

4. PERSEVERANCE

Carroll (1963) defines perseverance as the time the learner
is willing to spend in learning. Obviously, if a student needs to
spend a certain amount of time to master a task and he spends less
than this amount in active learning, he is not likely to master it.
In general, perseverance is related to student attitudes toward and
interest in learning (Husén, 1967). Students vary in the amount of
perseverance brought to a specific learning task. However, students appear to approach different learning tasks with different
amounts of perseverance owing, we believe, to the frequency of
reward and evidence of success they have experienced in the same,
similar, or related tasks. If a student has found his past efforts
rewarding, he is likely to spend more time on a particular task.
If, however, he was frustrated in his past learning, he must (in
self-defense) reduce the amount of time he devotes to the task.
While the frustration levels of students vary, all students sooner
or later must give up a task if it is too painful for them.
Perseverance is not fixed; it can be increased by increasing
the frequency of reward and evidence of learning success. Furthermore, the need for perseverance can be decreased by high quality
instruction. There seems to be little reason to make learning so
difficult that only a small proportion of students can persevere to
mastery. The emphasis should be on learning, not on endurance
and discipline for their own sake.

5. TIME ALLOWED FOR LEARNING

Throughout the world schools are organized to give group
instruction with definite time periods allocated for particular learning tasks. Whatever the time allowed, it is likely to be too much
for some students and not enough for others.
Assuming that aptitude determines the rate of learning, most
students can achieve mastery if they are allowed and do spend the
necessary amount of time on a learning task. There is little doubt

that students with high aptitude levels are likely to be more efficient and require less time for learning than students with lower
aptitude levels. Thus some students may need to spend six times
as much time as others to master a particular learning task. But
if both the instruction and students use time more effectively, this
ratio can be cut to perhaps three to one.

We are convinced, and the International Study (Husén, 1967)
supports our view, that it is not the sheer amount of time spent in
either school or extra-curricular learning that accounts for the
level of a student's learning. We believe the student should be
allowed the time he needs to learn a particular subject. The learning time needed will be affected by his aptitudes, his ability to
understand the instruction, and the quality of instruction he receives
in class and outside of class. An effective mastery learning strategy must find ways of altering the time individuals need for learning as well as providing the time necessary for each student. Such
a strategy, therefore, must solve the instructional as well as the
school organizational (including time) problems.

ONE STRATEGY FOR MASTERY LEARNING

Although there are many alternative strategies for mastery
learning, each must take into account the five preceding variables
in some way. Each strategy must deal with individual differences
in learners through some means of relating the instruction to their
characteristics and needs. A good tutor for each student would be
one ideal strategy, were it not so costly in terms of human resources. In any case, the tutor-student relationship is a useful
model to work with in attempts to develop a less costly strategy.

Recently a group at the University of Chicago has attempted
to develop a strategy for teaching and learning which will bring all
or almost all students to a mastery level in any subject. The
approach supplements regular group instruction by the use of diagnostic procedures and alternative instructional materials and methods so that a large proportion of the students can reach a predetermined standard of achievement within the regular term, semester,
or period of calendar time in which the course is usually taught.
Initial work has been done with subjects which have few prerequisites (such as algebra, science, and so on) because it seems
easier to secure mastery learning in a given time period in such
courses. Subjects which are late in a long sequence of learning
(such as sixth-grade reading, eighth-grade arithmetic, advanced
mathematics, and so on) were not used. It is unlikely that mastery
can be attained in a given term by students who have had a long
history of learning difficulties in such subjects. We have tried to

learn from both the successes and the failures we have had with this approach. Hopefully, in the near future some of these ideas will be applied to a large number of classes in selected school systems.

In developing this strategy, we have attempted to identify some of the necessary preconditions, to develop the operating procedures required, and to evaluate some of the outcomes.

PRECONDITIONS

If we want to develop mastery learning in students, we first must define mastery and then collect evidence to determine whether or not a student has attained it. In short, we must be able to recognize when a student has achieved mastery.

One necessary precondition is the specification of the objectives and content of instruction and the translation of these specifications into summative evaluation procedures so that both teachers and students understand what is expected of them in the teaching-learning process. These evaluation procedures inform both the teacher and the students when the instruction has been effective.

Implicit in this way of defining expectations and preparing evaluation procedures is a distinction between the teaching-learning process and the evaluation process. The teaching-learning process attempts to prepare the student in a learning area; the evaluation process attempt to appraise the extent to which this preparation has succeeded and development in the desired areas has been achieved. Both the teacher and the learner must have some understanding of the achievement criteria and both must be able to secure evidence of progress toward them

If the achievement criteria are primarily normative (i.e., the student is judged in terms of his relative position within the group), then the student must compete with others to determine his relative group standing. While competition may spur some students, much of learning and development may be destroyed if competition is the primary basis for motivation.

Much more preferable in terms of intrinsic motivation for learning are standards of mastery and excellence set in terms of what is to be learned and apart from inter-student competition. Absolute performance standards and the use of grades or marks to reflect attainment of these standards are suggested by this approach. Thus under a mastery learning system, it is entirely conceivable that all or none of the students may attain mastery and the grade A. Each student is appraised individually solely with respect to his performance vis à vis a fixed standard rather than his performance relative to a group of his peers.

While absolute standards carefully worked out for a subject are recommended, they are often difficult to set. One method might be to use standards derived from previous experience in a particular course. For example, grades for one year might be based on grading standards arrived at the previous year if parallel examinations are used. Students' grades would then be determined by performance relative to these standards rather than their rank order in the group. Students would not compete against each other for grades,and there would be no fixed proportion of students receiving any grade. This method has been used successfully in courses at the University of Chicago.

This is not the only way to arrive at achievement standards. However, the example illustrates the point that students must feel they are being judged in terms of their level of performance rather than by a normal curve or some other arbitrary and relative standard. We are not recommending national achievement standards, but realistic performance standards developed for each school or group followed by instructional procedures which will enable the majority of students to attain them. One positive result of this method of setting achievement standards is the emphasis on cooperative rather than competitive learning.

In the work we have done, we have attempted to teach the course in much the same way as previously in the belief that a useful strategy should be widely applicable and should not require extensive teacher retraining. We have used the same materials, methods of instruction, and time schedule. The courses have differed from the conventional ones only in the we have supplemented the regular instruction of the teacher in a unique manner.

OPERATING PROCEDURES

Our operating procedures have been designed to provide detailed information to both the teachers and students about the ongoing effectiveness of the teaching-learning process and to provide instructional correctives as needed. They ensure mastery of each learning unit in a shorter learning time by affecting the quality of each student's instruction and his ability to understand it.

FORMATIVE EVALUATION

One useful operating procedure we have employed is to break the course or subject into smaller units, such as a chapter in a textbook, a well-defined segment of content, or a particular unit of time. In general, we have tended to think of units as involving one to two weeks of learning activity.

We have used the ideas of Gagné (1965) and Bloom (1956) to analyze each unit into its constituent elements. These ranged from specific terms or facts to more complex and abstract ideas, such as concepts and principles. They even included complex processes, such as application of principles and analysis of complex theoretical statements. We have considered these elements as forming a hierarchy of learning tasks.

Given our description of the learning tasks for each unit, we have then constructed brief diagnostic-progress tests to determine which of the unit's tasks the student has or has not mastered and what he must do to complete his unit learning. The term "Formative Evaluation" has been borrowed from Scriven (1967) to refer to these instruments.

The formative tests are administered at the completion of each learning unit and thus help students pace their learning and put forth the necessary effort at the appropriate time. We find that the appropriate use of the tests helps ensure the thorough mastery of each set of learning tasks before subsequent tasks are started. While the frequency of these progress tests may vary throughout the course, it is likely that more frequent formative testing may be needed for the earlier units of the course than for the later ones since typically the early units are basic and prerequisite for all subsequent units. Where the learning of some units is necessary for the learning of others, the tests should be frequent enough to ensure thorough mastery of the former units.

For students who have thoroughly mastered the unit, the formative tests should reinforce their learning and assure them that their learning approach and study habits are adequate. The tests also should serve to reduce anxiety about end-of-course achievement for students who consistently demonstrate unit mastery.

For students who fail to master a given unit, the tests should pinpoint their particular learning difficulties - - that is, the specific questions answered incorrectly and thus the particular ideas, skills, and processes which need additional work. We have found that students respond best to diagnostic results when the diagnosis is accompanied by a very specific prescription of particular alternative instructional materials and processes they can use to overcome their learning difficulties.

Since formative tests are diagnostic, we believe they should not be officially graded. We have marked them simply mastery or non-mastery. We believe the use of grades on repeated formative-progress tests prepares a student to accept less than mastery. We have observed that when a student repeatedly receives C's, especially where the progress test grades form part of his final grade, then he is prepared to accept a C as his "fate" for the course. Once he believes that it is impossible to do better than a particular grade, he ceases to strive to improve his learning. Formative tests should be regarded as part of the learning process and not the judgmental or grading process.

Formative tests can also provide invaluable feedback to the teacher by identifying particular points in the instruction that are in need of modification. Also the tests may serve as a means of quality control in future replications of the course. The students' performance on each test can be compared with that of previous classes to ensure that they are doing as well or better and that new methods of instruction or new materials are not introducing new learning difficulties.

ALTERNATIVE LEARNING RESOURCES

By itself, the frequent use of formative progress tests can improve students' achievement to only a small degree. If, however, students can be motivated to correct their errors on these progress tests, then their achievement gains can be very great. The best way to motivate students to complete their learning is to provide specific suggestions (usually in connection with the formative evaluation results) as to what they need to do. We have found several types of corrective learning procedures to be effective. The best procedure seems to be small group study sessions in which two or three students meet regularly for as much as an hour per week to review their formative test results and to cooperatively overcome the difficulties these tests identified. We have also offered tutorial assistance, but secondary and college or university students do not seek this kind of help frequently. We have also prescribed other types of alternative learning resources, including a) rereading particular pages of the original instructional materials; b) studying specific explanations in alternative textbooks or other instructional materials; c) using specific pages of workbooks or programed materials; and d) using selected audio-visual materials.

Probably no specific learning material or process is indispensable. A great variety of instructional materials and procedures helps to assure the student that if he cannot learn in one way, alternatives are available. Hopefully, future research will discover the best match between certain types of individuals and alternative learning resources.

OUTCOMES

What are the results of a mastery learning strategy? So far, the evidence is limited by very encouraging. We are presently securing more evidence in a variety of subjects at all educational levels.

COGNITIVE OUTCOMES OF A MASTERY STRATEGY

Some of the most striking results of the effectiveness of a mastery learning strategy were found in a test theory course which used parallel achievement tests in 1965, 1966, and 1967. In 1965, before introduction of the mastery strategy, about 20 per cent of the students received A grades on the final examination. In 1966, the first year of the strategy's use, 80 per cent of the students reached the same mastery level on a parallel examination and were given A's. The highly significant difference in mean performance between these two groups represents about two standard deviations on the 1965 achievement test. In 1967, the 1966 formative evaluation tests became quality control measures. The instructor was thus able to spot specific difficulties and alter his explanation of the ideas during the progress of the course. The final results of the 1967 parallel final examination showed 90 per cent of the students had achieved mastery and were given A's.

Similar studies are being conducted at different educational levels. We expect to have many failures and a few successes. The important point, however, is not that a single mastery learning strategy can be used mechanically to obtain particular results. Rather, the task is one of ascertaining what procedures will help particular students effectively learn the subject under consideration. It is hoped that each time a strategy is used, studies will be made to find out where it is succeeding and where it is not. Who did it help and who did it not? Hopefully, each new year's efforts can take advantage of the experience accumulated over the previous years.

AFFECTIVE CONSEQUENCES OF MASTERY

For the past century, we have assumed that mastery of a subject is possible for only a minority of students. Thus we have adjusted our grading system to allow only a small percentage of students (no matter how carefully selected) to receive the grade of A. Even if a group of students learns to a higher level than a previous group, we still persist in awarding A's (or mastery recognition) to only the top 10 to 15 per cent. Only grudgingly do we acknowledge that the majority of students have "gotten by" by giving them D or C grades. Mastery and recognition of mastery is unattainable to the majority of students under the present relative grading system - - but only because of the way we have "rigged" the educational system.

Mastery must be both a subjective recognition by the student of his own competence and a public recognition by the school or society. Regardless of how much the student has learned, if he is denied public recognition in the form of appropriate certification by his teacher or school, he must come to believe that he is inadequate. Subjectively, the student must come to feel he has control over ideas and skills. He must come to realize that he "knows" and can do what the subject requires.

If the evaluation system (both formative and summative) and the grading system inform the student of his mastery of a subject, he will come to believe in his own competence. When he has mastered a subject and received both objective and subjective evidence of his mastery, there are profound changes in his view of himself and the outer world. Perhaps the clearest evidence of change is that he develops interest in the subject mastered. He begins to "like" it and desire more of it. To do well in a subject opens it up for further exploration; to do poorly, closes it. The student desires some control over his environment and mastery of a subject gives him some control over at least part of his environment. Interest in a subject then is both a cause and the result of its mastery. Motivation for further learning is an important result of mastery.

At a deeper level, subject mastery affects the student's self-concept. Each person searches for positive recognition of his worth and comes to view himself as adequate in those areas where he receives assurance of his success or competence. For a student to view himself in a positive way, he must be given many opportunities for rewards. Mastery and its public recognition provide the necessary reassurance and reinforcement. This writer believes that one of the more positive aids to mental health is frequent and objective indications of self-development. Mastery learning, therefore, can be one of the more powerful sources of mental health. We are convinced that painful and frustrating school learning experiences exacerbate many of the neurotic symptoms exhibited by high school and college students. One might expect that if 90 per cent of our students were given positive indications of learning adequacy, they would need progressively less in the way of emotional therapy and psychological help. Conversely, frequent failure and indications of learning inadequacy must occasion increased self-doubt in students and force them to search for reassurance and adequacy outside the school.

Finally, modern society demands continual learning throughout life. If the schools fail to promote adequate learning and to give students reassurance of their progress, then students will eventually reject learning, whether in school or in later life. Mastery learning can give zest to school learning and thus help develop a life-long interest in learning. It is this continual learning that should be the major goal of modern education.

REFERENCES

Atkinson, R. C. Computerized Instruction and the Learning Process. Technical Report No. 122. Stanford, California: Institute for Mathematical Studies in the Social Sciences, 1967.

Bloom, B. S. Stability and Change in Human Characteristics. New York: John Wiley & Sons, 1964.

Bloom, B. S. (ed.). Taxonomy of Educational Objectives: Handbook I, Cognitive Domain. New York: David McKay Company, 1956.

Bowman, M. J. "The New Economics of Education," International Journal of Educational Sciences, 1 (1966), 29-46.

Bruner, Jerome. Toward a Theory of Instruction. Cambridge, Massachusetts: Harvard University Press, 1966.

Carroll, John. "A Model of School Learning," Teachers College Record, 64 (1963), 723-33.

Congreve, W. J. "Independent Learning," North Central Association Quarterly, 40 (1965), 222-28.

Dave, R. H. "The Identification and Measurement of Environmental Process Variables that are Related to Educational Achievement." Unpublished Ph.D. dissertation, University of Chicago, 1963.

Gagné, Robert M. The Conditions of Learning. New York: Holt, Rinehart & Winston, 1965.

Glaser, R. "Adapting the Elementary School Curriculum to Individual Performance," In Proceedings of the 1967 Invitational Conference on Testing Problems. Princeton, New Jersey: Educational Testing Service, 1968.

REFERENCES CONTINUED

Goodlad, J. I. , and Anderson, R. H. The Nongraded Elementary School. New York: Harcourt, Brace, & World, 1959.

Hunt, J. McV. Intelligence and Experience. New York: Ronald Press Co. , 1961.

Husén, R. (ed.). International Study of Educational Achievement in Mathematics: A Comparison of Twelve Countries, Vols. I and II. New York: John Wiley & Sons, 1967.

Morrison, H. C. The Practice of Teaching in the Secondary School. Chicago: University of Chicago Press, 1926.

Schultz, T. W. The Economic Value of Education. New York: Columbia University Press, 1963.

Scriven, Michael. "The Methodology of Evaluation," In Perspectives of Curriculum Evaluation. Edited by Robert Stake. Chicago: Rand McNally & Co. , 1967.

Skinner, B. F. "The Science of Learning and the Art of Teaching," Harvard Educational Review, 24 (1954), 86-97.

Suppes, P. "The Uses of Computers in Education," Scientific American, 215 (1966), 206-221.

Chapter 5

OPERATING PROCEDURES FOR MASTERY LEARNING

James H. Block

A pervasive and vexing problem for teachers and administrators has always been the transformation of new and promising ideas into school practices. Many ideas have been developed without the classroom in mind and thus have defied implementation. This has not been the case with mastery learning. Successful classroom strategies have been easily and inexpensively developed both in this country and abroad. To stimulate further development efforts, this chapter outlines the major operating procedures found most effective in past mastery learning strategies.

A POINT OF VIEW

The research summarized under category G of the Bibliography establishes that, under appropriate conditions, almost all students can learn a given subject up to a mastery level. Acceptance of the view that almost all students can learn to high levels is basic to the development of an effective strategy for three reasons.

First, the view's acceptance stimulates teachers, administrators, and, ultimately, students to strive for high levels of learning. It shifts the burden of primary responsibility for student performance from the student to the school system. The net effect of this shift is to commit school personnel and resources to creating

instructional conditions under which almost all pupils can learn
well.   Teachers and administrators are encouraged to use their
resources as effectively and efficiently as possible to meet their
commitment.   As this commitment is met each student becomes
convinced through new school policies and practices that he can
learn, and he overcomes any feelings of defeatism he may have
brought to his learning.   Students begin to like their mastery
learned subjects and desire to learn more about them.

Second, the view's acceptance provides a touchstone for the
solution of most procedural problems encountered during a strategy's development and/or its implementation.   Whenever difficulties arise, appropriate solutions can be found by asking which
course or courses of action are likely to promote the learning of
all, not just some, students.

Third, its acceptance helps justify modification of school
grading policies and practices so that all students who attain mastery can be appropriately rewarded for their efforts.   As long as it
is assumed that almost all cannot learn well or that some can learn
better than others, the major problem is to sort the capable from
the incapable students.   By limiting the number of academic rewards (e.g., high grades) given, the traditional grading system
creates the competition required for separating those who learn
easily from those who do not.

However, when it is assumed that almost all can learn to high
levels, the problem becomes not to sort students out but to ensure
that all do learn to the levels expected.   Here a limited number of
rewards is counterproductive.   In a system with few rewards, a
student may not be rewarded no matter how well he learns so long
as others learn better.   If this situation occurs repeatedly, he is
likely to eventually stop trying to learn well.   In a system of un-
limited rewards, by contrast, a student who learns well can be
rewarded even though others may learn still better.   Successful
and rewarding learning experiences are likely, in turn, to kindle a
desire for continued learning excellence.

SELECTING SUBJECTS FOR MASTERY LEARNING

Once this view is accepted, the subject or subjects can be
selected for which a mastery strategy will be developed.   Past
mastery learning research has focused on particular subjects at
all levels of education (elementary, secondary, and higher).   A
review of this work shows that mastery approaches have produced
best results in subjects possessing some and frequently all of the
following characteristics.

The subjects have required either minimal prior learning or

previous learning which most learners already possessed. For
example, mastery methods have been more effective for first-grade
arithmetic and ninth-grade algebra than eighth-grade arithmetic.
The learning of first-grade arithmetic requires little, if any, previous arithmetical training, and the learning of algebra requires
only simple arithmetical skills which most students have acquired
by the ninth grade. The learning of eighth-grade arithmetic, however, requires the arithmetical skills of grades one through seven,
which many students may not possess.

The success of mastery strategies in subjects requiring little
or no prior learning is easily explained. Their learning depends
primarily on the quality of the instruction. Since mastery procedures produce instruction of optimal quality for each learner, they
ensure that most students will learn very well. The learning of
subjects requiring much prior learning, however, depends upon
both the student's possession of the prerequisite learning and the
quality of the instruction. While again mastery approaches can
make their instruction of optimal quality, they might not be able to
offset the negative effects of deficient prior learning.

Mastery learning strategies also have been most effective for
subjects which are sequentially learned. Such subjects consist of
a number of well-defined units whose learning is cumulative in that
the learning of any unit builds upon the learning of all prior units.
For example, reading is usually learned sequentially. Each chapter in a first-grade reader builds upon the vocabulary and syntac-
tical structures presented in the preceding chapters. Similarly,
the first chapter in the second-grade primer is likely to assume a
student's familiarity with all the material learned in the first-grade.

The success of mastery learning strategies in sequentially
learned subjects is also easily explained. The learning of any
sequential subject depends upon the learning of each of its units.
If at each stage in the sequence the student learns the material
upon which the next unit builds, then his learning throughout the
sequence is likely to be adequate. However, if he fails to learn at
one stage and his learning difficulties are not resolved, he will
probably fail to learn the unit at the next stage and, consequently,
all subsequent units. Mastery approaches, by means of supplementary feedback/correction procedures, ensure sufficient learning
of each unit and hence adequate learning of the entire subject.

Finally, the subjects in which mastery learning strategies are
most effective have tended to be closed and to have emphasized
convergent rather than divergent thinking. As defined by Bloom
(1971), closed subjects are composed of a finite set of ideas and
cognitive behaviors about which both curriculum makers and
teachers concur. They are also subjects whose content has not
changed, and is not likely to change, for sometime. English and

arithmetic, for example, would be closed subjects. Subjects which emphasize convergent thinking are those in which students are taught to obtain appropriate answers or solutions through accepted problem solving modes (e.g., arithmetic) (Guilford, 1959).

The success of mastery approaches in these types of subjects may be attributed to the consensus regarding what students are to learn and how they are to learn it. This consensus makes it easier to define mastery and to measure students' attainment of it.

While we believe that an entire mastery learning curricula should be developed, most schools will want to experiment on a smaller scale with one or more subjects. Mastery learning has worked for subjects (e.g., philosophy) (Moore, Mahan, and Ritts, 1968) possessing other characteristics than those mentioned above. But for relatively quick and clear demonstrations of its powerful effects, subjects possessing the preceding characteristics are recommended. Early courses in basic required subjects (e.g., arithmetic, English, reading, mathematics, and science) are good candidates. Typically, required subjects are sequential and closed and emphasize convergent thinking. Highly sequentially structured subjects such as algebra, chemistry, and physics might also be recommended. Foreign languages are also possibilities. The more alien the language to English (e.g., Russian), the better the results are likely to be.

DEFINING AND MEASURING MASTERY

As Bloom (1968) first pointed out, to develop mastery in each student's learning, teachers must be able to recognize when students have attained it. One necessary step in this direction is to specify the objectives of instruction in terms of skills (content as well as cognitive processes) the student is expected to learn. The crucial step, however, is the translation of these objectives into specific summative evaluation procedures whereby the evidence required to judge and grade each student's learning at a subject's completion can be gathered. The translation of skills to be learned into skills to be tested helps teachers clarify precisely what skills the students are expected to learn. The summative instrument's items, therefore, operationally define mastery in terms of a specific set of skills each student is expected to have learned by the subject's completion.

Many procedures have been used and can be recommended for summative evaluation purposes. Perhaps the best are those instruments cooperatively constructed directly from agreed upon instructional objectives by teachers in the subject to be learned for mastery. The derivation of the instrument or instruments from the pre-defined objectives ensures that they are content relevant for the subject and objectives under consideration. Less preferable, but equally possible, instruments are the final examination and/or progress tests from either a previous or a concurrent teaching of the subject under non-mastery conditions. If there is concern about repeating the same examinations, parallel tests might be constructed. Finally, standardized tests can be used if they are clearly relevant to the subject and the instructional objectives.

As we pointed out at the beginning of this section, summative evaluation will only provide evidence regarding a student's learning of the expected skill. To completely operationally define mastery, therefore, it is necessary to establish an absolute performance standard against which the sufficiency of each pupil's learning can be judged and graded. This standard should indicate the specific proportion of skills tested a student must exhibit before he can be judged to have mastered the subject. It should be absolute in the sense that it is set prior to the summative evaluation and serves as the sole criterion against which each student's performance is judged.

There are no hard and fast objective rules for setting mastery grading standards. Until such rules become available, only those standard setting methods found useful in the past can be recommended. One method is to set the standard subjectively. If this method is used, the standard is perhaps best set cooperatively by both teachers and administrators. Mastery learning procedures ensure that most students will attain any standard. When this occurs and teachers alone have set the grading standard, they become worried that administrators will reject the standard; administrators, in turn, become worried that teachers have lowered the standard. A grading standard set cooperatively by both parties should reduce anxiety considerably.

A second standard setting method is to transfer existent grading standards set for the subject under non-mastery learning conditions to the courses taught under mastery conditions. Standards from previous or concurrent non-mastery teachings of the subject can be used. Generally, scores which earned students learning under non-mastery conditions A's and B's seem to be useful mastery grading standards.

Regardless of how the standard is set, we must reemphasize that once set, it must be used as the sole criterion for judging student performance. Neither teachers nor administrators need feel they have gone "soft" by giving perhaps almost all students A's under an absolute grading system compared to only 10 to 20 per cent under a relative grading system. The normal curve is not sacrosanct. By grading each student solely on the basis of his performance vis à vis an absolute rather than relative standard, one simply reestablishes the relationship between performance and reward that was lost when the curve began to be used.

In a relative grading system there may be little relationship between performance and reward because each pupil's reward is contingent on the performance of others. Regardless of how well he learns, if others learn better, he will not receive the highest grades. Conversely, regardless of how poorly he might perform, if others perform less well, then he will receive the highest grades. In an absolute grading system, however, performance and reward are integrally related. The grading standard is defined in performance terms, and the student is rewarded on the basis of his performance compared to the standard. Hence, if mastery learning helps almost all students to learn to the same high performance levels which earned A's for the top 10 to 20 per cent under non-mastery conditions, then an absolute grading system can give legitimate A's to almost all students.

FORMATIVE EVALUATION

Summative evaluation can assess a student's achievement at the end of instruction, but it cannot help guide the teaching-learning process. For this purpose some kind of evaluation which can provide immediate and continuous information regarding a student's progress during instruction is required. Here formative evaluation has been found to be most useful (Airasian, 1969).

Formative evaluation is designed to be an integral part of the teaching-learning process. The instruments are brief, so that they do not take up inordinate amounts of instructional time. They are also diagnostic. Each instrument tests those skills students must learn from a given instructional unit if they are to master the major desired skills. A formative instrument administered at the close of a unit, therefore, provides an in-depth picture of what skills each student has or has not learned. Consequently, it suggests in what ways his original instruction must be supplemented if he is to complete his learning before proceeding to a new instructional unit.

Since the following chapter by Dr. Airasian focuses on the full role of formative evaluation in mastery learning and the construction of formative instruments, let us turn directly to those operating procedures which have made the use of formative evaluation most effective. One such procedure has been to break the subject to be learned into smaller instructional or learning units before constructing the instruments. These units have usually corresponded to chapters in a textbook, two weeks' instruction, or well defined topics. These short units keep the formative instruments brief:

if fewer skills are learned per unit, fewer skills must be tested. Short units also mean more frequent testing. This facilitates the detection and subsequent correction of learning difficulties before they seriously impair later learning. The frequent testing also helps pace student learning. Students are pressed to put forth appropriate learning effort throughout the subject rather than just at its completion, when even great learning efforts may be too little, too late.

A second valuable operating procedure has been not to grade the formative instruments. Frequent graded tests might lead some students to think they could do work of only a particular caliber and discourage them from striving for learning excellence. To provide motivation, however, it has been found useful to mark each student's unit tests with non-grade designations such as "mastery" or "more work needed." The "mastery" marking gives those who receive it positive evidence of their academic achievement. This evidence reinforces their approach to the learning, suggests their study habits are satisfactory, and may even generate positive interest in and attitudes toward the learning. The "more work needed" marking encourages students to complete their unit learning. This has especially been the case when they have been convinced that per unit learning "mastery" almost guarantees their mastery performance on the summative instrument.

Marking the formative tests in this way requires the establishment of a per unit performance standard in addition to the summative mastery grading standard. Typically these standards have been set subjectively, but cooperatively, by the teachers responsible for carrying out the mastery strategy. Recently, though, more objective empirical standard setting procedures have been developed (Block, 1970). The empirical work to date suggests that if students learn 80 to 85 per cent of the skills in each unit, then they are likely to exhibit maximal positive cognitive and affective development as measured at the subject's completion. This work also suggests that encouraging or requiring students to learn all or nearly all (90 to 95 per cent) of each unit, besides being an unrealistic expectation in terms of student and teacher time and effort (Bormuth, 1969), may have marked negative consequences for student interest in and attitudes toward the learning (Block, 1970; Sherman, 1967).

Finally, formative test results can be used most effectively when each student's performance is interpreted in terms of his response to each test item. Each item represents a skill the student was to have acquired from the relevant instructional unit. If only his total formative test score is considered, therefore, one obtains information on how much the student learned but throws away information on what he did or did not learn. Only this latter information can guide the teaching-learning process.

The teacher, by examining student responses to each test item, can spot those which gave a majority of the class problems. Given this information, he can determine the material to be reviewed for the entire class before moving on to the next instructional unit. The teacher may also be able to discover the root of each student's particular learning problems. He can then prescribe the specific learning correctives each student requires to quickly complete his unit learning.

The student, by examining his correct and incorrect item responses, is provided with a detailed profile of his learning progress. He can see what skills he has learned and what ones remain to be learned. Rather than wasting precious time reviewing the whole learning unit, he can focus his attention on the particular content, concepts, and processes still unmastered.

LEARNING CORRECTIVES

The feedback provided by formative evaluation instruments to both teacher and student can only promote the latter's learning so far. To promote student learning to the fullest extent, therefore, the diagnostic information provided by formative evaluation must be translated into specific supplementary instructional procedures whereby each pupil can correct his particular unit learning difficulties. As pointed out in Chapter 1, the purpose of these correctives is to provide each learner with the clearest and most appropriate instructional cues, the requisite amounts of active involvement in and practice of the learning, and the amounts and types of reinforcements his learning requires.

Presently there are no methods for going from a student's incorrect formative test responses to the specific learning correctives he needs. For this reason, a wide variety of instructional correctives have been made available so that the student can discover those best suited to his characteristics and needs. The following are the correctives which have been most effective.

SMALL GROUP PROBLEM SESSIONS. Perhaps of all the correctives, small group problem sessions involving three to four learners with very different difficulties have worked best with elementary school children. Typically, these students lack both the independence and the perseverance required to complete their learning by themselves using alternative instructional or learning materials. The sessions provide a specific block of time when students are formally constrained to attempt to complete their learning. In the small groups each child is given a chance to teach and be taught by others of his own age. We find that the children have a remarkable ability to cooperatively correct each other's learning errors.

INDIVIDUAL TUTORING. Probably the most efficient and effective method for correcting individual learning problems for either younger or older students is individual tutoring. At the college or university level, the costs of tutoring are minimal because students who have previously mastered the material are readily available for use. Unfortunately, however, at the elementary and secondary school levels, where student tutors are less available, the cost of tutoring is so high as to preclude its use unless other correctives are not available. If tutoring can be obtained, it should ideally be done by someone other than the teacher who brings new perspectives to the student's instruction.

ALTERNATIVE LEARNING MATERIALS. For older students, who possess both the independence and the perseverance to correct their learning problems by themselves, the provision of a number of alternative learning materials has proved to be especially effective. Typically, the materials used are those the school already owns or can easily acquire.

Alternative Textbooks. Often the textbook adopted for course use is not of consistently high quality in explaining particular points and processes. Alternative textbooks can be used to fill in these gaps. It has been found useful, therefore, to have delimited for each formative test item sections in other textbooks where the skill tested by the item is explained in a variety of ways. The greater the variety of explanations, the more likely it is that each student will be able to find the presentation best suited to his characteristics and needs.

Workbooks and Programed Instruction. For learners who have great difficulty grasping ideas and processes from a highly verbal type of instruction (e.g., students with hearing handicaps), workbooks and programed instruction are especially useful. Workbooks provide the drill and the specific problem solving practice the students need for learning. Programed instruction provides small learning steps and immediate and frequent reinforcements.

Audio-Visual Methods. For students who have difficulty grasping material presented in a verbal-abstract instructional mode, audio-visual methods are useful. Film strips, motion pictures, classroom demonstrations, and instructional illustrations provide these students with clear, concrete explanations of the material they are expected to learn.

Academic Games and Puzzles. Little work has been done using academic games and puzzles, but so far results indicate they are especially useful for students who view learning for learning's sake to be sheer drudgery. Games and puzzles provide these students with another incentive to learn (Coleman, 1967). Learning is instrumental to the attainment of a specific goal - - winning the game or solving the puzzle.

Reteaching. In some cases a large number of students fail to learn particular skills either because they originally were not taught or were only superficially taught. This situation can usually be discovered by taking simple hand counts of the number of students who missed each formative test problem. When deficiencies are discovered, it has been found useful to reteach them to the entire class. If certain skills were mistakenly skipped over in the original instruction, then the originally planned instructional mode can be used. If they were only superficially taught, however, then it is useful to present the material in a new instructional mode.

It must be emphasized that the correctives described in this section are intended to supplement and not to replace the original instruction and instructional materials. They may be viewed as crutches to be used by a student at those particular points where his original instruction was not of optimal quality. Once his instruction becomes optimal, they can be discarded until needed again.

THE FREQUENCY OF USE OF THE FEEDBACK/CORRECTION PROCEDURES

As we have seen, the major intent of formative feedback and learning correction devices is to pinpoint and correct student learning deficiencies before they impair subsequent learning. Depending on the relevance of the learning of particular units in a subject to the learning of others, it may be necessary to use feedback/correction devices more than once in a given learning unit. This is especially likely for the earliest units in any subject, whose learning is almost always fundamental to the learning of later ones. In the case of sequentially learned subjects, the learning of the skills in the early units is necessary, but not sufficient, for the learning of the skills in later units. In the case of both sequentially and non-sequentially learned subjects, the student's success or failure on the early units shapes his interest in and attitude toward the learning of later units. For such subjects, more frequent use of the feedback/correction devices during their early units would ensure each student's thorough mastery of the skills and provide him the successful initial learning experiences crucial for sustaining his desire to learn.

THE ALLOCATION OF LEARNING-INSTRUCTIONAL TIME

Given the already limited amount of instructional time

available, the reader at this point is probably asking himself where time can be found for each student's unit correction/review. If students are to complete their learning on their own time, then it is probably only necessary to give them access before and/or after school to the corrective materials. Perhaps they might be allowed to use the materials for an hour or two or to check them out to work on at home.

If students are to complete their learning on school time, however, then there are at least two major courses of action that can be taken. One is to reschedule classes so that each student is allowed enough total learning time (original instruction time plus correction/review time). This procedure has worked very effectively at the college and university levels. The other, which necessitates no flexible or modular scheduling and should be most effective at the elementary or secondary level, is to simply redistribute the instructional time available in the following special way.

Teachers usually break their instructional load into a number of smaller units and then allot uniform amounts of instructional time per unit. For example, two weeks might be alloted to each chapter in a fifteen-chapter textbook. Recent research (Block, 1970; Merrill, Barton, and Wood, 1970) begins to suggest, however, that if the teacher sets aside more instructional time for the earlier units, then he will have to spend less time than usual on the later units. The total amount of instructional time spent for a course under this arrangement will be no more and probably less than he would have spent under the usual system.

The allotment of more time for the early units ensures that each pupil is allowed the correction/review time necessary to learn these units thoroughly. The research indicates that thorough learning of early units results in more efficient and effective learning of later units. Progressively smaller amounts of correction/review time are required. The net effect of these changes is that students require less and less total (original plus correction/review) instructional time per unit to maintain a high level of learning performance.

STUDENT ORIENTATION

In mastery learning research, it has been found that a sizeable number of students are so convinced they cannot learn to high levels that they are unwilling to give the feedback/correction procedures a chance to promote their learning. In attempting to carry out successful mastery strategies, therefore, it has proved useful to set aside the first class period to attempt to convince all students they can learn the subject. During this period, students have been told of the strategy's goals and the methods to be used in attaining them. The following points have been stressed:

1) The student will be graded solely on the basis of his final (summative) examination performance.

2) The student will be graded on the basis of his performance vis à vis a predetermined standard and not relative to his peers.

3) All students who attain the standard will receive appropriate grade rewards (usually A's) and there will be no fixed number of rewards. (So that students do not feel their rewards are debased, since everyone can get them, it has been useful to state the grading standard and to explain its meaning in terms of the performance of students learning under a non-mastery system.

4) Throughout the learning, the student will be given a series of ungraded, diagnostic-progress tests to promote and pace his learning.

5) Each student will be given all the help he needs to learn. (Here it has been effective to indicate the various learning correctives so that the student is convinced that if he can not learn one way, other ways are available.)

This orientation period, combined with encouragement, support, and positive evidence of learning success, especially early in the subject, usually will develop in almost all students the belief that they can learn and the instrinsic motivation to learn.

CONCLUDING REMARKS

This paper has listed the major operating procedures that have been found most useful in developing and carrying out mastery learning strategies. Hopefully, new strategies and further research will produce additional procedures.

REFERENCES

Airasian, Peter W. " Formative Evaluation Instruments: A Con-
struction and Validation of Tests to Evaluate Learning Over
Short Time Periods. " Unpublished Ph. D. dissertation,
University of Chicago, 1969.

Block, James H. " The Effects of Various Levels of Performance
on Selected Cognitive, Affective, and Time Variables. "
Unpublished Ph. D. dissertation, University of Chicago, 1970.

Bloom, Benjamin S. " Learning for Mastery, " UCLA-CSEIP
Evaluation Comment, 1 , No. 2 (1968).

Bloom, Benjamin S. "Mastery Learning and Its Implications for
Curriculum Development, " in Confronting Curriculum Reform.
Edited by Elliot W. Eisner. New York: Little, Brown and
Company, Inc. , 1971

Bormuth, John R. Development of Readability Analysis. Final
Report. USOE, Contract No. OEC-3-7-0700052-0326, 1969.

Coleman, James S. "Academic Games and Learning, " in Proceedings of the 1967 Invitational Conference on Testing Problems. Princeton, New Jersey: Educational Testing Service, 1968.

Guilford, J. P. Personality. New York: McGraw-Hill, Inc. , 1959.

Merrill, M.D., Barton, Keith, and Wood, Larry E. "Specific
Review in Learning a Hierarchical Imaginary Science, "
Journal of Educational Psychology, 61 (1970), 102-09.

Moore, J.W., Mahan, J.M. , and Ritts, C. A. " An Evaluation
of the Continuous Progress Concept of Instruction with
University Students. " Paper read at the annual meeting of
the American Educational Research Association, Chicago,
February, 1968.

Sherman, J. G. " Application of Reinforcement Principles to a
College Course. " Paper presented at the annual meeting of
the American Educational Research Association, New York,
February, 1967.

Chapter 6

THE ROLE OF EVALUATION IN MASTERY LEARNING

Peter W. Airasian, Boston College

Mastery learning (Bloom, 1968) attempts to accommodate individual differences between learners to promote the fullest development of each learner vis à vis a set of stated instructional goals. Instruction is individualized within the context of regular group instruction by means of on-going, specific feedback about each student's learning progress, coupled with a variety of corrective instructional modes to help the pupil learn material unmastered during group instruction.

While there are other approaches to individualized instruction (Cronbach, 1967), all depending upon sound, relevant information for their effective functioning, no approach relies as heavily upon constant information flow for its success as does mastery learning. In mastery learning, evidence gathering is a crucial and integral aspect of the instructional process itself. Without constant information to identify weaknesses in student learning, there can be no effective strategy. The remainder of this paper is concerned with the types of information needed to carry out mastery learning and with the procedures applicable to obtaining that information.

EVALUATION IN MASTERY LEARNING

An effective mastery strategy requires two types of evaluation.

On the one hand, it demands constant, on-going formative evaluation to provide information useful for directing student study and
teacher practice. The evaluation is formative in the sense that it
is utilized to indicate how students are changing with respect to
their attainment of the instructional goals. On the other hand, an
effective strategy also requires summative or end-of-instruction
evaluation, primarily to grade student achievement. Such evaluation provides information about how students have changed with
respect to the course aims.

The use here of different verb tenses to describe formative
and summative evaluation is intended to indicate the degree of
finality associated with evaluative evidence from the respective
approaches. Formative evaluation provides data about how students
are changing. The verb tense indicates that the process designed
to foster change is still occurring and that evaluative evidence can
be useful in fostering further change. Summative evaluation is
concerned with how students have changed. The implication is that
the changing process is for the most part completed and that little
correction of identified deficiencies is possible. Both formative
and summative evaluation are related to instruction, and both seek
to appraise changes in learner behavior. However, the different
purposes of formative and summative evaluation call for different
evaluative procedures.

SUMMATIVE EVALUATION

In mastery learning, the primary purpose of summative
evaluation is to grade students according to their achievement of
the course aims. Summative evaluations are in the realest sense
"final" and grades assigned on their basis are likely to follow the
student throughout his scholastic career. Summative examinations
occur infrequently, typically covering relatively large blocks of
instructional material. The use of the term "relatively large" is
admittedly vague and most frequently will take its specific meaning
from teacher practice.

While many types of data are useful for grading purposes,
summative evaluation instruments are usually paper and pencil
tests designed to appraise the extent to which the larger, more
general course objectives have been attained. Summative scoring
can be in terms of individual item responses or sub-scores (by
objective, teacher emphasis, and so on), but since terminal,
sorting information is the primary end, a total score is usually
employed. An accurate means of ranking students with respect to
their mastery of the overall course objectives is sought. Those
who attain the pre-defined mastery level receive an A grade or

some other suitable indication of mastery performance. Those who fail to attain the mastery level receive appropriately lower grades.

Summative evaluation adequately fulfills one of the two functions evaluation is called upon to perform in a mastery strategy. It is an efficient, usually accurate, and reliable means of grading student achievement. However, summative evaluation is ill-suited to perform the second evaluative role of providing on-going evidence, during the instruction, to identify learning weaknesses to be corrected prior to grading. A single, summed score obtained at the conclusion of a lengthy instructional segment may inform teachers that their students have failed to master some objectives, but a single score neither pinpoints the locations of non-mastery nor suggests appropriate corrective measures. Further, unmastered objectives are identified too late to provide students the opportunity or incentive to correct their errors. The opportunity has fled because summative evaluations, due to their relative infrequency, their inclusion of only a sub-set of the material covered, and their scoring characteristics, neither locate the precise point in instruction where students went wrong nor aid students in learning the subsequent material whose mastery depended upon learning the unmastered material. The incentive to undertake corrective measures is diminished because a summative evaluation certifies performance and produces a grade. Mastering certain points missed in a summative evaluation may give a student satisfaction, but it does not raise his grade. To overcome these limitations, formative evaluation was conceived.

FORMATIVE EVALUATION

Formative evaluation provides the information necessary to individualize instruction within a mastery strategy. Basically, formative evaluation seeks to identify learning weaknesses prior to the completion of instruction on a course segment - - a unit, a chapter, or a lesson. The aim is to foster learning mastery by providing data which can direct subsequent or corrective teaching and learning. Thus formative evaluation is an integral part of the instructional process.

In keeping with its aim, formative evaluation should occur frequently during instruction. It should strive to identify unmastered learning areas early enough to permit their correction before the grading evaluation. If learners must wait one or two or more months to discover that they have not mastered a concept introduced in the first week of instruction, being informed of such errors benefits them little. Students need to be informed of their non-mastery at a time when they can, if they choose or if the instructional mode permits, correct their errors. Conducting frequent formative evaluations to identify unmastered objectives is especially useful in subjects where material introduced in the early stages of instruction forms the basis for learning later material.

To carry out adequate formative evaluation, the evaluators (e.g., teachers) must be cognizant of the classroom practices and emphases. Such an awareness is required because formative procedures, if they are to provide relevant and specific information, must be derived from the instructional activities preceding the evaluation. For example, it makes little sense to evaluate students' ability to synthesize the material they have been taught when the stated aim of instruction and the instructional method itself stressed only memorization of specifics. In addition, variability in teaching emphasis or classroom goals must be taken into account if formative evaluation is to provide accurate and useable data in particular settings and over a number of course cycles.

Given such awareness, the actual techniques of formative evaluation can take many forms. Perhaps the most common form - - although it is seldom recognized as such - - is teacher observation. Almost all teachers gather what can be termed formative evidence during their instruction. Teachers implicitly select and respond to cues from their pupils. They barely acknowledge one pupil's question yet painstakingly respond to another's because they know that the former pupil can find the answer on his own, whereas the latter has encountered prior difficulties mastering similar concepts. They ignore one student's raised hand and select another's because they feel that the latter pupil requires recognition and reinforcement in his learning. Teachers respond to other cues, such as shifts in posture, tones of voice, momentary facial expressions, types of questions, and the like, which, although less formal than other techniques available, are used to appraise the on-going success of instruction.

Although teacher observation represents the most prevalent form of information gathering during instruction, its lack of rigor presents some difficulties. A primary difficulty is that teachers may not respond to a representative sample of their students. Some of our recent research, in which we have interviewed a small sample of teachers about their expected instructional outcomes, indicates that many instructors prejudge what certain pupils are capable of learning. For example, a number of the instructors we interviewed, at all grade levels, suggested that only the most intelligent or motivated students are able to learn at a level higher than strict recall. Not only do such prejudgments contradict the mastery learning philosophy, but they are likely to

limit the type of student from whom teachers accept cues. A
question from a low intelligence or poorly motivated learner may
be dismissed by the teacher because he has the ready-made rationale, "This student can't learn that anyway." Whether or not
teachers accept cues from a representative sample of their students
may also depend on factors such as a pupil's mode of dress, his
perceived social class, and the performance of older brothers and
sisters taught by the same teacher. In addition to the problem of
representativeness, legitimate questions can be raised about the
reliability of teacher observations as well as the standards utilized
to judge the meaning of the observations.

    If formative evaluation is to serve its purpose of providing
on-going information about learning while instruction is in progress,
more formal evidence gathering procedures are needed. One
method for collecting suitable formative evidence involves evalu-
ating all objectives in a unit, chapter, or lesson which are prerequisite to mastery of other objectives in the unit, chapter, or
lesson. For example, an algebra chapter might have as one of its
ultimate objectives "to solve unfamiliar word problems by means
of simultaneous equations." Items which evaluate learning of this
overall objective would suffice for a summative evaluation. However, mastery of the general objective implies that students have
mastered a series of prerequisite objectives, for example, "to
solve simultaneous equations," "to translate word problems into
equations," and so on. If grading is the prime intent of evaluation,
data about performance on the more general objective is adequate;
but if the evaluation is intended to identify learning weaknesses
prior to grading, evidence about the student's ability to perform
each prerequisite objective should be obtained.

    One approach to formative evaluation attempts to analyze
short units of learning with the aim of identifying not only the
objectives to be learned, but also the relationships between objectives (Airasian, 1971a). The first step in the analysis involves
identifying the new content presented in the unit, chapter, or lesson under consideration. New content is defined in terms, facts,
rules, skills, types of problems, syntheses, and so on, which have
not been introduced to students in prior units, chapters or lessons.

    With the new content identified, the second step in the analysis
involves specifying the level of mental or cognitive operation necessary to learn each content element. In most units of instruction,
some things are to be memorized, others are to be understood so
that the student can express them in his own words, still others
are to be utilized in solving new and unfamiliar problems, and so
on to higher and higher levels of cognitive functioning. Each
element of content must be analyzed in terms of the cognitive operation the student will be required to perform if he is to master it.

For example, assume that one of the new content elements to be learned in a Civil War unit is the war's outcomes. Some instructors may expect their students simply to memorize the outcomes. Others may expect their students both to memorize the outcomes and to explain them in their own words. Still others may expect both memorization and explanation, but they may further stress the use of these cognitive behaviors to analyze events in succeeding historical eras. One convenient and useful scheme for identifying different types of cognitive operations is the Taxonomy of Educational Objectives - Cognitive Domain (Bloom, et al., 1956). The taxonomy presents a series of cognitive operations hierarchically organized into levels according to their complexity.

The third step in the formative process involves positing relationships between content to be learned at the different cognitive levels. It should be decided which content elements to be learned by simpler mental operations are necessary, but not sufficient, prerequisites for mastering other elements to be learned by more complex operations. In our Civil War example, it should be clear that a student must remember the outcomes before he can explain them in his own words. Similarly, he must be able to explain the outcomes in his own words before he can use them to analyze events in post-Civil War eras. Consequently, for a teacher who expects memorization, explanation, and analysis from his students, a hierarchy of related outcomes can be specified. The outcomes represent the objectives of the unit and are stated in terms of a content element to be learned and the cognitive behavior necessary to learn it. The hierarchy begins with the simplest level of cognitive operation (memorization) and ends with the most complex (analysis). Mastery of each objective in this hierarchy is dependent upon mastery of all preceding objectives.

In more general terms, defining relationships between content to be learned at different levels of cognitive operation involves inspecting content at the most complex level and asking what content, if any, at the next lower level the student must know in order to learn the higher level content. If no content at the next lower level is judged prerequisite, the third lower level is inspected and the same question asked. This process in continued until a relationship is found between content at the most complex level and content at a less complex level, or until the less complex levels are exhausted. Having dealt with content at the most complex level, the process is repeated for content at successively less complex levels. Research has shown that with a little practice, teachers working independently can reach a high level of agreement on the hierarchy of outcomes contained in units of learning material (Airasian, 1970).

The hierarchies produced by following the steps summarized

TABLE 1

Summary of Steps Utilized to Define a
Hierarchy of Outcomes

Step 1	Identify content elements (terms, facts, rules, syntheses, skills, types of problems, etc.) which have not been introduced to students in prior lessons, chapters, or units.
Step 2	Define the level of cognitive functioning (memorization, explanation, application, analysis, etc.) necessary for a student to master each new content element.
Step 3	Specify relationships between content elements at different levels of cognitive functioning. The relationships should indicate which content elements at simpler levels are prerequisite to learning content at more complex levels.

in Table 1 provide a teacher with information to answer such questions as "Does this unit place too much emphasis on recall or remembering behaviors as opposed to more complex behaviors?" or "Where can I build relationships into this material to facilitate learning and transfer as my student progress through more and more complex levels of mental operation?" Hierarchies of outcomes provide a map for planning instruction and supplementing existing curriculum materials to produce instruction compatible with teacher aims.

However, the prime function of hierarchies is to provide a blueprint for the construction of the evaluation instrument. Once a unit has been analyzed, items to evaluate learning of each content element at the appropriate level of cognitive functioning can be constructed or selected. Without a prior, detailed description of what is to be learned, it is difficult to collect an appropriate set of items to evaluate learning. Here, the term "item" should be interpreted to mean a method of obtaining information about a specific learner capability. In this light, numerous evidence gathering forms and procedures may be useful for collecting formative data. For example, one might formatively evaluate a chemistry, math, or history learning unit by means of paper and pencil tests composed of multiple-choice or fill-in items. By the same token, to evaluate an individual's ability to swim the back-stroke, build a bookcase, or fix a leaky drain, an observation check-list based upon the hierarchy of skills needed for successful performance may be used. Regardless of the type of formative instrument or the form of the items, at least one item to test each element in the hierarchy must be included in the instrument. If some outcomes in the hierarchy are not evaluated, specific diagnosis of learning difficulties will be incomplete.

There is one exception to this maxim. In some instructional segments, the objectives may be non-hierarchical and unrelated to one another. In such cases value judgments must be made regarding which objectives to include in the formative instrument. The criteria for making such value judgments are many, but can include the value placed on the particular objective, the amount of time devoted to it during instruction, its perceived future value both outside the course and as a basis for learning material in subsequent course segments, and the extent to which it organizes learning in prior course segments.

After a formative instrument has been administered, it should be scored in terms of item response patterns so that each unmastered objective can be identified. For the purposes of formative evaluation, a single score hides more than it reveals. If two students answer the same number of items correctly on a summative evaluation, their grades are usually identical. It matters little that one student answered only recall items correctly, while the other answered only more complex items correctly. Since formative evaluation focuses on informing students and teachers about learning deficiencies early enough in instruction to permit corrective action, formative information must be appropriate to this end. Patterns of item responses permit each student to identify readily those objectives he has failed to master. The student is afforded a very specific portrait of his performance vis à vis the hierarchy of objectives of the learning unit.

The teacher should collate individual student data on each formative item to find out which objectives the class as a whole had trouble learning. Objectives not mastered by a large percentage of the class, about 40 per cent or more, generally warrant reteaching rather than individual correction. On objectives only a small percentage of the group fails to master, individualized remediation can be stressed. In either case, the hierarchy of objectives provides a strategy for corrective activities. Correction should proceed from the lowest level in the hierarchy where learning difficulty was manifested to the highest level, since mastery of each higher level element requires mastery of the related lower level elements (Airasian, 1971b).

Formative procedures incorporating hierarchies of objectives and scored in terms of item response patterns provide both students and teachers with a clear delineation of those objectives mastered, those not mastered, and the relationship between what has been mastered and what is yet to be mastered. Such detailed information further indicates the optimal level at which to begin correction of unmastered material. Correction is made more efficient insofar as the student is provided specific directions, such as "learn to remember the definition of density" or "learn to state in your own words the meaning of the word 'democracy'" or "learn to translate word problems into equations," rather than the more general and less useful "work harder," "restudy the chapter," and the like.

Somewhere between relatively informal teacher observation and the more formal procedures just discussed, rest a number of other potential sources of formative information. These additional sources derive principally from data teachers usually have at hand: homework papers, classroom test results, standardized test results, and the like. However, if such data are to be useful in a formative sense, they generally must be put into another form. For example, the total score, grade equivalent, or percentile rank on either a standardized or teacher-made achievement test is of little formative value because it does not provide specific enough information about the objectives a student has or has not mastered. The teacher must inspect item response patterns - - or at the very least sub-scores on the test - - to determine what specific objectives the student has mastered relative to the ultimate objectives of the instruction. Similarly, for homework papers to provide formative information, the teacher must be able to specify why a student answered a problem incorrectly, so that specific corrective activities can be prescribed. If this information is not available or cannot be deciphered given the problem and the student's response, little direction is given for correcting learning difficulties.

The point is that most of the additional data sources teachers have available are designed to perform a function other than providing formative information. As a consequence, they are not specific enough to be used as formative instruments without appropriate modification. If the information about what has been learned and what has yet to be learned in a given course segment is not precise and individualized, it is extremely difficult to maintain a mastery strategy within the context of on-going group instruction. Students will be unable to correct their errors and return to regular group instruction with any degree of efficiency. Of course, there is nothing to prevent homework exercises or classroom tests from being developed to incorporate hierarchies of objectives along the lines suggested above.

Regardless of the type of formative evaluation instrument used, students must be free to make mistakes without being penalized. Formative evaluation is part of the learning process and should not be confused with assigning final grades. The use of grades on formative evaluations can have two undesirable effects. First, repeated failing grades soon convince students that they are in fact failures. They are likely to assume the attitudes and behaviors of an academic failure. Second, if formative results are averaged into the final grade, students ultimately reach a point where no matter how hard they try, they cannot raise their final average. Both of these consequences defeat the prime purpose of formative evaluation and mastery learning.

In addition to being ungraded, formative tests should be designed to reduce the time lag between the evaluation and the use of the evaluation's results. Instantaneous feedback is required because the mastery strategy is carried on within the context of on-going group instruction. As a consequence, formative information must be received and acted upon quickly so that individualized correction can occur before regularly scheduled group instruction is continued. To wait days or weeks for the results of a formative test destroys the rhythm of the classroom and severly hampers the opportunity for success of the mastery strategy. Identification of learning deficiencies must occur during or immediately subsequent to instruction on a course segment so that corrective action can take place prior to the introduction of new material or the grading examination.

One strategy for quickly identifying unmastered objectives is the use of special answer sheets which have a place for the student to mark his answer to each formative item, a list of remedial activities (workbook pages, film strips, programed texts, and so on) keyed to each item in the formative test, and a diagram showing the hierarchy of objectives for the course segment being evaluated. Since formative evaluations are not graded, students can score their own answer sheet immediately following administration of the formative instrument. By referring to the diagram of the hierarchy provided on the answer sheet, each student can identify those objectives he has mastered and those he has not yet mastered. For each unmastered objective, the student can refer to the list of corrective activities keyed to each item and undertake the one or ones he selects to correct the deficiency. By obtaining a hand count from the class as a whole for each formative item, the teacher can determine the objectives not mastered by a sufficiently large proportion of the class to warrant reteaching rather than individual correction. Such procedures permit formative results to be acted upon with a minimum of delay. Further, they permit each student to correct his own deficiencies by selecting his own corrective materials.

The busy teacher responsible for the functioning of large and varied classes will seldom have time to carry out individually the steps required in a formal system of formative evaluation. This recognition should not be interpreted to suggest that teachers abandon a formal formative evaluation system in favor of the more spontaneous and informal practices which have been utilized for so long. Cooperative efforts by groups of teachers are needed. Such collaboration should involve a number of teachers, yet place minimal time demands on any single teacher. We have found that teams of three or four classroom teachers working approximately three hours a day can define hierarchies, construct test items, and locate appropriate corrective exercises for all chapters in typical algebra, chemistry, and biology textbooks in about ten weeks. While the time used by these teachers may represent a lower bound on the time needed to construct a formal formative evaluation system, the point to be emphasized is that groups of teachers working together can design and construct formative evaluation instruments and answer sheets in a relatively short time.

The benefits of formative techniques for both teachers and students are many. Formative testing is a means of pacing student learning. By dividing an entire learning sequence into smaller segments and by pressing students to study while they are being taught a particular segment, formative evaluation prevents students from postponing their study until they are faced with an overwhelming amount of material to learn in a short time. In addition, formative results either reinforce students' mastery over a course segment or provide a very specific indication of those objectives still to be mastered. In either case, the student is informed frequently about his learning progress. If the objectives in a segment are hierarchically ordered, students who have not attained mastery are afforded a strategy for sequencing their corrective activities.

Formative evaluation also can inform teachers of the class' learning progress over short segments of instruction. Such information can be utilized to alter instruction or to review those ideas which students had difficulty mastering. Formative procedures provide a measure of quality control for the teacher in that they permit the examination of student learning progress with respect to the teaching techniques employed to facilitate their learning. Finally, the use of formative evaluation casts the instructional process in the light of a system where teacher and students cooperate rather than oppose each other as adversaries.

CONCLUDING REMARKS

This paper has endeavored to introduce a number of concepts which help define the role of evaluation in an effective mastery learning strategy. It has attempted to indicate that the role evaluation can play in the educational process is not limited only to the collection of evidence for grading student achievement. The major portion of the discussion dealt with formative evaluation, its place in the learning process, and its potential applications. If the reader carries away no more from this paper than the realization that evaluation procedures can be utilized to enhance the teaching and learning processes in a variety of ways, it will have been successful.

REFERENCES

Airasian, Peter W. "The Use of Hierarchies in the Analysis and Planning of Chemistry Instruction," Science Education, 54, No. 1 (1970), 91-95.

Airasian, Peter W. "The Use of Hierarchies in Curriculum Analysis and Instructional Planning," California Journal of Educational Research, 1971a (in press).

Airasian, Peter W. "A Study of Behaviorally Dependent, Classroom Taught Task Hierarchies," Educational Technology, 1971b (in press).

Bloom, Benjamin S. "Learning for Mastery," UCLA-CSEIP Evaluation Comment, 1 (1968). (Whole No. 2).

Bloom, Benjamin S., et al. Taxonomy of Educational Objectives, Handbook I: Cognitive Domain. New York: David McKay Co., Inc., 1956.

Cronbach, Lee J. "How Can Instruction Be Adapted to Individual Differences?" in Learning and Individual Differences. Edited by Robert Gagné. Columbus, Ohio: Charles E. Merrill Books, Inc., 1967, pp. 23-39.

PART TWO

AN ANNOTATED BIBLIOGRAPHY

ON

MASTERY LEARNING

INTRODUCTION

This bibliography draws together some of the relevant literature on mastery learning. It is intended for use by both teachers,
administrators, and research specialists. For this reason, each
abstract is more detailed than is usually the case. Hopefully, the
greater detail will assist the reader in drawing some implications
from the reported findings, in posing some important questions,
and in suggesting possible future research. The interested reader,
of course, should return to the original sources for a more complete presentation of the ideas.

The bibliography is not intended to be a complete summary
of the relevant literature. Only those empirical and, in some cases,
theoretical papers have been abstracted which most clearly point
out some of the fundamental concepts and variables to be considered
in the development of mastery learning strategies.

We have tried to follow a consistent form in presenting the
abstracts. In so far as possible, each one contains the following
information:

1) the major question, problem or purpose of the study;

2) the procedures and/or design;

and 3) the major findings and conclusions.

In some cases, the editor has appended additional summary or interpretive comments. These are intended to point out the relevance and implications of the study for mastery learning.

Further, to facilitate use of the bibliography, we have classified each entry by relating it to the major variables in the mastery learning model. Each abstract has the letters A through G in the upper-right hand corner to indicate which of the following categories is most relevant:

A. Aptitudes and rate of learning

B. Ability to understand instruction

C. Quality of instruction

D. Perseverance

E. Time as a variable in attaining mastery

F. Affective consequences of school learning

G. Use of mastery concepts and strategies

Some abstracts are indexed by more than one letter. The first letter indicates the abstract's primary focus.

In preparing this bibliography, the editor asked specialists working on particular aspects of mastery learning to write some of the relevant abstracts. Those persons who have contributed either summaries of their own work or abstracts of relevant works in their own or related fields of interest are as follows:

Peter W. Airasian (Boston College)
Benjamin S. Bloom (University of Chicago)
Kenneth M. Collins (Purdue University)
Mildred E. Kersh (University of Washington)
Hogwon Kim (Seoul National University)
Christopher Modu (Educational Testing Service)
Kay Torshen (University of Illinois, Chicago)
Robert Wise (Stanford University)
William J. Wright (Central Midwestern Regional Educational
Laboratory)

These individuals' initials appear at the end of their abstracts.

SUMMARY OF MASTERY LEARNING RESEARCH

To provide an overview of the research results described in the Bibliography, the following brief summaries have been prepared.

A. Aptitudes and Rate of Learning

The research indicates that students differ in the rate at which they learn a given subject or learning task and that a students' learning rate may vary from subject to subject or task to task. On many standardized achievement tests, selected criterion scores achieved by a minority of students at one grade level are achieved by the majority only at later grade levels. Studies of programs in which student learning is self-paced suggest that the slower pupils may require five to six times as long as the faster to master a set of learning materials.

Aptitudes, as measured by either standardized aptitude tests or simple pretests of a student's prior knowledge of a subject, are predictive of not only the level to which a pupil will learn in a given time, but also the amount of time he will require to learn to a given level. There is some evidence that aptitudes predict learning rate because they are the most simple and general learning skills or entry behaviors for a given subject or task. Many subjects and learning tasks can be analyzed into a hierarchical series of intellectual skills where the learning of the lower level skills is a necessary, but not sufficient, precondition for the learning of the higher level skills. Aptitudes are most clearly predictive of student learning rate for the initial or lower level skills. In turn, the learning of the lower level skills is predictive of the learning rate of the higher level skills.

Generally, different aptitudes predict student learning rate in different subjects although a few, such as verbal ability, predict learning rate across many content areas. One of the major remaining research problems is the identification of the aptitudes most relevant for a given learning task.

B. Ability to Understand Instruction

The findings indicate that the same subject or learning task, depending on the instructional mode in which it is taught, may require very different aptitudes. Since most school instruction tends to be highly verbal, a basic variable in the student's ability to

understand instruction is his verbal ability or intelligence. Verbal
ability correlates significantly with student learning rate and
achievement for most school subjects. Generally, it is also the
single best predictor of grades in elementary and in secondary
school.

Aptitude-Instructional Treatment Interaction research suggests
that by modifying the instructional mode in which a subject is first
presented to fit the learner's aptitudes, a teacher can optimize both
the level of his achievement and his learning rate. Similar results
can be obtained more easily by supplementing the student's group-
based instruction with a variety of feedback/correction devices.
Regardless of the approach used to increase a student's ability to
understand instruction, the evidence is clear that the use of only a
single mode of instruction hampers the learning of students who
are weak in the aptitudes required to learn in that mode.

C. Quality of Instruction

The research results suggest that quality of instruction is best
defined by a) the clarity and appropriateness of the instructional
cues for each student; b) the amount of participation in and practice
of the learning by each pupil; and c) the amount and types of reinforcements given to each learner. Related to these variables are
the findings that the variety of instructional modes and materials,
teacher verbal ability, the type of feedback available to both teacher
and student, and the frequency and variety of teacher reinforcements are all predictive of student achievement.

The quality of instruction affects both student learning rate
and achievement level. In terms of learning rate, poor quality
instruction makes the learning of students who have difficulty in
understanding the instruction more inefficient. High quality instruction, however, makes all students' learning more efficient. In
terms of level of achievement, poor quality instruction seems to
impair the learning of both high and low intelligence students although the high I.Q. students may be least affected. That is, students of higher intelligence may be able to learn in spite of poor
instruction. Extremely high quality instruction operates to help
most students to achieve to approximately the same high levels in
spite of differences in intelligence, aptitudes, or entry behaviors
brought to the learning. The findings suggest, in fact, that the
instruction is defective to the extent to which students' individual
differences in intelligence, aptitudes, or entry behaviors are reflected on the achievement measure.

Two major methods have been used to improve the quality of
instruction with respect to each student's ability to understand.

One method, represented by Aptitude-Instructional Treatment Interaction research, attempts to construct instructional methods and materials to fit different student's aptitude patterns. For example, if a student is high in verbal and low in spatial aptitudes, then a verbal presentation is suggested. Conversely, if a student is high in spatial and low in verbal aptitudes, then a presentation emphasizing the use of graphs, models, and concrete demonstrations is suggested. This method to date has produced little clear evidence of significant changes in student achievement.

A more promising, and far less expensive, approach supplements the usual group-based instruction with feedback/correction procedures. The feedback devices (e. g. , formative-diagnostic tests) are built into the instruction to point out deficiencies in student learning of a given instructional segment and to suggest the alternative instructional correctives required to overcome them. The most effective correctives have included reteaching of selected aspects of an instructional segment, small group cooperative study sessions, individualized tutoring, and the provision of various alternative instructional methods and materials students can use on their own. Essentially, the correctives attempt to provide each student with the instructional cues, the learning participation-practice, and the reinforcements which are best suited to his characteristics and needs, but which he did not receive at particular points in the group-based instruction. The evidence begins to suggest that effective feedback/correction procedures can transform classroom instruction of any initial quality into instruction of optimal quality for each learner. Student achievement is significantly improved and the overall time spent in learning a series of tasks may be markedly less than that required where the instruction does not provide feedback/correction procedures.

D. Perseverance

Of all the mastery learning variables, perseverance is the one about which there are the least data. The research does identify an individual trait called persistence (i.e., the ability of keeping on at a task) which is distinct from either simple endurance or an involuntary inability to shift one's train of thought. Students do differ in their persistence for a particular kind of learning task - - probably because of their history of prior success or failure on similar or related tasks.

The research demonstrates that persistence may be increased by some form of external positive reinforcement (e. g. , rewards) or learning success. It also may be increased or decreased by the quality of instruction. High quality instruction appears to increase the persistence of students of high and low intelligence, but it seems to have little effect on the persistence of those of average intelligence.   Poor quality instruction may lead to less persistence in any student.

E.   Time as a Variable in Attaining Mastery

Under both the traditional instructional programs, where classes are given periods of fixed length, and the newer individualized programs, where time is variable and learning is self-paced, it is clear that students differ in the amount of time needed to learn a given subject to a mastery level.   As pointed out in summary A, this is most evident in the self-paced programs, where the faster students master materials five to six times as quickly as the slower. Further, the same student may require quite different amounts of time to learn different subjects.   If he is not allowed the time he needs for a particular subject, his learning is likely to be incomplete.   Conversely, if he is allowed enough time, his learning will be complete and his achievement will be raised.

A student's learning rate for a given subject or learning task can be predicted by his aptitudes as measured by either standardized aptitude tests or by simple pretests.   Given the relationship between learning rate and aptitudes, there have been an increasing number of attempts to construct instructional strategies that will take advantage of each learner's aptitudes and hence increase his learning rate.   The most successful strategies have supplemented group-based, classroom instruction with feedback/correction procedures. If a school subject is presented as a sequence of learning units, then thorough mastery of the earliest units, with the help of feedback/correction devices, will make student learning of later units more effective, efficient, and progressively less dependent on these devices.   While more instructional time than usual must be invested to ensure that the early units are thoroughly mastered, this additional time is likely to be saved in the learning of the later units. The total amount of instructional time used in this way will be no more, perhaps even less, than that used in traditional instructional methods where uniform amounts of instructional time are alloted per learning unit.

F.   Affective Consequences of School Learning

The research findings reveal a clear, perhaps causal, relationship between a student's academic performance and progress and both his self-concept and his mental health.   Self-concept and

ego development derive in part from the individual's perception of
the evaluations that significant people make of him. For the student, the teacher is one such person. Teacher grades have a much
stronger effect on a student's self-concept and mental health than
do quasi-objective evaluations based on his standardized test performance. Even as late as the freshmen and sophomore years of
college, if a student's grades change dramatically compared to his
high school marks, then there are accompanying changes in certain
of his personality characteristics. Teacher grades are apparently
one of the major types of evidence by which students judge themselves.

The results also suggest that if a student can be provided with
a history of successful and rewarding experiences in a given type
of task, his confidence in his ability to perform similar and related
tasks will increase, his aspiration to learn will be heightened, and
his actual performance will improve. Successful and rewarding
experiences across a number of subjects can lead to the development of intrinsic motivation for further general learning. Finally,
consistent success in school learning over a number of years may
constitute a type of immunization against anxiety and emotional
disorders.

G. Use of Mastery Learning Concepts and Strategies

All mastery strategies are designed to take into account
individual differences among learners in such a way as to promote
each student's fullest cognitive and affective development. Typically, they accomplish this task by manipulating either the learning
time allowed each student and/or the quality of his instruction
through various feedback/learning corrective devices.

The results from almost 40 major studies carried out under
school conditions indicate that mastery learning has marked effects
on student cognitive and affective development and their learning
rate. In general, mastery strategies enable about three-fourths
of students to learn to the same performance standards as the
top fourth of students learning under conventional, group-based
instructional approaches. The strategies seem to be especially
effective for those students who typically have had problems learning under ordinary instructional conditions. For example, students
with below average I.Q. scores seem to learn as well under mastery conditions as students with above average I.Q. scores under
a traditional approach. For subjects where most of the students
have achieved the prerequisite learnings, mastery procedures
appear to be able to almost eliminate the effects of individual differences on level of achievement.

Mastery methods also produce markedly greater interest in and better attitudes toward the material learned than more conventional approaches. They seem to help most students overcome feelings of defeatism and passivism brought to the learning. Their powerful affective consequences may be attributed to many factors, the most important of which seem to be the cooperative rather than competitive learning conditions, successful and rewarding learning experiences, personalized attention to each student's learning problems, and the use of certain correctives (e.g., student tutors and small group study sessions) which add a personal-social aspect to the learning not typical of group-based instruction.

Finally, mastery approaches also make student learning increasingly efficient. Mastery of the earliest units in a school subject appears to facilitate the learning of the subsequent units, especially where the learning units are sequentially arranged. The instructional time spent to ensure adequate learning over the first units in the course seems to result in the need to spent less time than usual over the later units to maintain a high level of student performance.

G, E

Airasian, Peter W. , 1967.
"An Application of a Modified Version of John Carroll's Model of
    School Learning. "
Unpublished Master's thesis, University of Chicago.

This study reports an attempt to apply a modified version of
Carroll's "Model of School Learning" to a graduate level course in
test theory.   The intent was to produce mastery of the subject in
the largest proportion of students (n = 33) within a ten week learning period.

The course was broken into five learning units, each covering
approximately two weeks of learning activity.   Upon completion of
each unit, the students were given short diagnostic-progress (formative evaluation) tests.   These tests were not graded and were
intended to provide feedback to both the teacher and the students on
the adequacy of the teaching-learning process.   For students who
had mastered the content of the unit, the tests indicated their mastery and the adequacy of their study habits; for those who did not
attain mastery on each unit, the test pointed out specific weaknesses
and prescribed alternative learning resources or study modes by
which these difficulties could be overcome.   Commonly missed
items indicated points of weakness in the instruction which the instructor corrected before moving on.   Time-Study Inventories
provided bi-weekly indications of each student's study-time allot-
ments.   Mastery over all the course content was measured by the
student's achievement on a graded final examination.

The main result was striking.   Whereas in the previous year
only 30% of the students received an A grade, 80% of the sample
achieved at or above the previous year's A grade score on a parallel
exam and thus received A's.   Two other results were also of interest.   First, the correlation between total hours of weekly study and
achievement was slightly negative.   The author attributes this
finding to the effectiveness of the feedback system in apparently
leveling initial differences in prior exposure to the course materials.   The diagnostic tests seemed to make all students use study
time more efficiently by identifying important course aims and
behaviors.   Second, there was less variability over time in achievement on the formative evaluation instruments.   In spite of the
varying backgrounds possessed by the subjects, this strategy was
effective in bringing most of the students to a high degree of
achievement by the end of the course.

(P.W.A.)

G, C

Airasian, Peter W. , 1969.
"Formative Evaluation Instruments: A Construction and Validation
     of Tests to Evaluate Learning Over Short Time Periods. "
Unpublished Ph. D. dissertation, University of Chicago.

The problem investigated involved both constructing formative
evaluation instruments and investigating their properties. The
instruments were defined as tests designed to be administered over
short time periods to provide information to the curriculum con-
structor, teacher, and students regarding the adequacy of the
teaching-learning process.

Using some of the ideas of Gagné and Bloom, two curriculum
specialists in algebra and two in chemistry analyzed two chapters
from a textbook in their respective areas into a number of elements
ranging from specific terms or facts to relatively complex processes such as the application of principles or the analysis of
theoretical statements. These elements were assumed to fit a
hierarchical model in which learning of the content elements at the
lower behavioral levels was viewed as necessary, but not sufficient,
for learning content elements at higher behavioral levels. These
hierarchies were translated into formative tests by constructing
items to test each element at the appropriate level in the hierarchy.
One hypothesis was that students who failed an item testing a lower
level element in the hierarchy would fail all related higher level
items. Approximately 60 algebra students and 130 chemistry students took part in the study.

The main findings were as follows. First, in each subject
area, the two independent curriculum experts reached over 90%
agreement in defining the elements included in the instructional
unit and in identifying the hierarchical relations among the elements.
This result supports the idea that learning hierarchies can be
found in certain learning materials. Further, if such hierarchies
can be identified, it suggests that a set of items which possess
content validity can be derived from these hypothetical hierarchies
to evaluate the actual structure and relationships inherent in the
learning unit. Second, generally more than 75% of the students'
response patterns on the formative tests conformed to the hypothesized hierarchical model. That is, students who missed lower
level elements in the hierarchy also missed the related higher
level items.

The author goes on to discuss the uses of formative evaluation
procedures in the development of curricula, the individualization
of instruction, and strategies of mastery learning.

(P. W. A.)

C, G

Anthony, Bobbie C. M. , 1967.
"The Identification and Measurement of Classroom Environmental
  Process Variables Related to Academic Achievement. "
Unpublished Ph. D. dissertation, University of Chicago.

  Using observational and interview techniques, an attempt was
made to identify aspects of the classroom environment hypothesized to influence academic achievement. A carefully selected,
representative sample of 21 classes in ten schools were rated on
51 process characteristics from six observations of each class and
supplemental interviews with the teacher. These were all fifth-
grade classes. In addition to the educational environment measurements, pre- and post-achievement measures and initial intelligence
measures were obtained.
  The partial correlation of the Educational Environmental Index
with post-achievement averages was +. 64, with prior achievement
held constant. Similar results were found when the Educational
Environmental Index was based on 14 selected process characteristics instead of the total group of 51 process characteristics. It
is of interest that the 14 variables can be grouped into three sub-
groups:

1. The variety of instructional materials and techniques used
  in the class.

2. The types of feedback available to teachers and students
  about the effectiveness of both teaching and learning.

3. The frequency and variety of reinforcements used by the
  teacher.

(B. S. B.)

* * * *

  The editor regards the relationship between achievement and
the variety of instructional material and techniques as indicating
the importance of using a variety of instructional approaches to
improve the quality of instruction. These data also suggest that
the use of feedback by teachers and students is necessary to adapt
the quality of instruction and remediation to learners. Finally,
these findings demonstrate that the use of frequent and varied reinforcements is also important in the production of optimal quality of
instruction needed for greater learning.

E, G, C

Atkinson, Richard C. , 1968.
"Computer-based Instruction in Initial Reading. "
In Proceedings of the 1967 Invitational Conference on Testing Pro-
    blems.   Princeton: Educational Testing Service, pp. 55-67.

This paper describes the reading phase of Stanford's Computer
Assisted Instruction Program (CAI) and presents some results for
the first year.   CAI attempts to deal with individual differences in
reading by means of tutorial programs based on applied psycho-
linguistics and tailored to the strengths and weaknesses of the student by computer.   Each lesson is composed of a number of "main
line" problems which the student must master before he can go on
in the program.   The computer monitors the student's responses
and provides new problems or remedial materials accordingly.

The results for the sample of first graders indicate great
variability in the rate at which students learn under self-paced
learning conditions.   If the number of "main line" problems completed during a seven month period is taken as an index of rate of
learning, the median student completed approximately 2,500 problems.   The slowest student, however, completed approximately
1,000 problems, while the fastest completed about 5,000 - - approximately a one-to-five ratio.   Further, the number of problems
completed on a per-hour basis per month during the course of the
year increased steadily for the fastest student, while it remained
relatively constant for the slowest student due to the amount of
remedial material.   The data also show that CAI students, on the
average, performed significantly better than a control group in
terms of reading achievement at the year's end.

The conclusion drawn was that CAI responded to individual
differences from the standpoint of both the total number of problems
completed and rate of progress during the year.   For example,
while it is commonly found that girls acquire reading skills more
rapidly than boys, under CAI there was no significant difference in
rate of progress between males and females.

*   *   *   *

The editor believes that the highly controlled conditions
offered by Computer Assisted Instruction will provide basic data
for a useful theory of instruction.   The work reported here also
makes it clear that students can achieve mastery of each task, although at different rates.   The variation in time required (5 to 1)
poses one of the main problems for mastery learning strategies - -
how to reduce time variations in learning by improvement in quality of instruction and the use of feedback/correctives at strategic
points in a learning sequence.

G, F

Ausubel, D. P. , 1964.
"How Reversible Are the Cognitive and Motivational Effects of
 Cultural Deprivation ? Implications for Teaching the Cultur-
 ally Deprived Child. "
Urban Education, 1 (1964), 16-38.

This paper focuses on the problem of reversing the retarda-
tion in the development of intelligence and motivation associated
with cultural deprivation. The author proposes that the learning
deficits found in culturally deprived children are caused by the lack
of opportunities to learn necessary skills during the early years of
development. The lack of these skills limits the benefits obtained
from later environmental stimulation. His review of the literature
indicates that abstract thinking, test-taking skills, vocabulary
skills such as familiarity with specific vocabulary, and level of
motivation are significantly affected areas.
    To compensate for these learning deficits, the author recom-
mends emphasis on mastery in the teaching-learning process. In
this approach the child's state of readiness for dealing with the
instruction to be presented should be considered. The student
should be presented with sequentially arranged learning tasks
appropriate to his level of development. Finally, each task should
be mastered before the next task is attempted. The child's successful achievement should provide the basis for the development of
intrinsic motivation for learning.
    (K. T.)

B, C, A

Behr, Merlyn J. , 1967.
"A Study of Interactions between 'Structure-of-Intellect' Factors
 and Two Methods of Presenting Concepts of Modulus Seven
 Arithmetic. "
Unpublished Ph. D. dissertation, Florida State University.

The major purpose of this study was to examine the possibility
of designing instructional materials to fit learners' mental ability
profiles. Two programs dealing with addition and subtraction and
some structural properties of modulus seven numbers were constructed and randomly assigned to 228 university students. One
program used figural means and the other verbal means to present
the material. The amount of symbolic material presented in both
programs was held constant. For example, in the Figural-Symbolic
(FS) program a model was used to present the operations of addition and subtraction; in the Verbal-Symbolic (VS) program, verbal

rules were used. A battery of aptitude tests which might interact with these instructional methods and the learning materials was given prior to the administration of the programs. Three criterion measures were used: time to study the program and achievement and retention test scores.

Several significant interactions between the instructional methods and the mental ability factors were found. Three verbal factors significantly predicted scores on at least one of the criterion measures for the Verbal-Symbolic, but not for the Figural-Symbolic, treatment group. Similarly, one figural factor significantly predicted time used to study the program by the FS, but not by the VS, group. A fourth verbal factor (cognition of semantic relations) also interacted with the two methods of instruction, but in a way contrary to expectations: it significantly predicted time used to study the program for the FS, but not for the VS, group.

*   *   *   *

These results are noteworthy for several reasons. They point out that instructional materials can be constructed to fit the strengths and weaknesses of the individual. People who are high in certain given abilities are likely to perform better if the material is presented in a mode which emphasizes those abilities. Similarly, persons who are low in certain abilities may actually be put at a disadvantage if the mode of presentation stresses those abilities. Also, the interactions between abilities and method with respect to the time used to study the program suggest that it should be possible to construct instructional methods which both <u>maximize</u> each learner's performance and <u>minimize</u> the time he requires to obtain optimal performance.

G

Biehler, Robert F., 1970.
"A First Attempt at a 'Learning for Mastery' Approach."
<u>Educational Psychologist</u>, <u>7</u>, No. 3, 7-9.

A mastery learning strategy for teaching introductory undergraduate educational psychology is reported on in this paper. The strategy's purpose was to reduce examination pressure and competition among students, to counteract the negative impact of poor early test performance on a student's subsequent learning, to maintain a respectable level of student learning, and still to assign grades within an A-to-F system.

Students were given the option of learning under either a traditional letter grading system or a mastery grading system. The mastery option included the following features. A list of key points (course objectives) was drawn up and circulated among the students to give them an idea of what they were expected to learn. The list also served as a base for the construction of three unit tests. Each test was normatively graded, and a score above which students ordinarily would have received A or B grades was defined as the unit mastery performance standard. Students who failed to attain the standard on each test could review and then take an alternate test form. To give students an opportunity to examine topics of their own choosing, three brief papers and a term paper were required. These papers could be resubmitted if their original quality was found to be insufficient. Final grades were assigned on the basis of mastery/non-mastery on the unit tests and the submission (or resubmission) of acceptable papers.

Only anecdotal results were reported. The strategy seemed to be especially effective, both cognitively and affectively, for students whose performance on the first course examination might ordinarily have led them to give up. These students found that they still had a chance to do well in the course if they were willing to spend additional review time and retake the test. The procedure has been revised for subsequent use. Over 90% of the students registered for the new course have chosen to learn under the mastery rather than the letter grading option.

C, A, E, G

Block, James H., 1970.
"The Effects of Various Levels of Performance on Selected Cognitive, Affective, and Time Variables."
Unpublished Ph.D. dissertation, University of Chicago.

The purpose of this study was twofold. First, a rationale for setting objective, criterion-referenced performance standards for sequential learning tasks was proposed, applied, and validated. Second, the cognitive and affective consequences of requiring students to maintain particular mastery levels throughout the learning of a sequential task were examined.

Eighth graders (n = 91) were taught three sequential units of elementary matrix algebra over a school week. The students were randomly assigned to five groups. The control group (n = 27) learned the algebra under no requirement that they maintain any per unit mastery level. Each of the remaining groups learned the units to a different, pre-established level - - 65, 75, 85, or 95 per cent mastery. Per unit performance was measured by formative tests administered at each unit's completion. Feedback/correction-review procedures helped students maintain their required mastery level throughout the learning. For each pupil the following measures were taken: pre- and post-achievement and transfer, retention, total learning time per unit (including time spent in correction/review), and interest in and attitudes toward the algebra at various stages during the instruction and two weeks after its completion. The pretest and Metropolitan scores on reading and arithmetic served as indices of individual differences in student algebra entry resources.

There were several major findings. First, maintenance of the 95 per cent mastery level produced maximal cognitive learning (achievement, transfer, and retention) but had long run negative effects on student interest and attitudes. Maintenance of the 85 per cent level produced maximal interest and attitudes, but slightly less than optimal cognitive learning. The maintenance of both the 85 and the 95 per cent levels, however, produced significantly greater cognitive learning than the maintenance of no per unit mastery level. These data suggest, therefore, that some care must be taken in the selection of the mastery levels students are asked to maintain throughout their learning. The maintenance of one level (e.g., the 95 per cent) may have opposite effects on cognitive and affective development. The data also imply that a mastery level can be selected which, when maintained, will maximize positive development of the desired learning - - cognitive as well as affective.

Second, the maintenance of a high level of per unit mastery can make student learning increasingly efficient. By Unit Three, those in the 95 per cent group learned substantially more material, even without the use of the unit's feedback/correction-review procedures, than the control group. But the two groups spent the same amount of unit learning time. The data trends indicate that if there had been additional learning units, most students in the 95 per cent group would have been able to maintain their high mastery level virtually without need for spending time with the feedback/correction procedures. Like a crutch, these procedures might have been eventually discarded.

Finally, despite the individual differences in the entry resources (pretest and previous achievement measures) of students in the 85 and 95 per cent groups, these differences were not reflected in their final achievement. Most students in each group learned to approximately the same high level. Further, while their resources played a large role in the learning of the first unit, they played a decreasing role in the learning of subsequent units. For control students (who maintained no unit mastery level), however, the resources played a large role in their final achievement and in their learning throughout the sequence. That is, entry resource measures were predictive of student learning under usual instructional procedures, but not under the mastery learning conditions used.

These findings suggest that the use of feedback/correction procedures to supplement the original instruction is a key to the transformation of ordinary group-based instruction into instruction of optimal quality for each student in the class.   The results also raise some pertinent questions about the role of individual differences in classroom learning.   They suggest that individual differences need not condition student learning and that perhaps individual differences have largely been used as a scapegoat for ineffective instruction.

F

Brookover, Wilbur B. , Shailer, Thomas, and Paterson, Ann, 1964. "Self-concept of Ability and School Achievement. "
Sociology of Education, 37, 271-78.

This study was based on the view that a person's self-concept is developed through his interaction with persons who are important to him and that these interactions, in turn, influence his future behavior.   It focused on one aspect of the student role, academic achievement, and one aspect of self-concept, self-concept of academic ability, and asked how these two aspects interrelate.

Two forms of a Self-Concept of Ability Scale were administered to a sample consisting of 1,050 seventh graders (half male and half female).   One form measured general self-concept and the other measured self-concept in each of four specific school subject areas: arithmetic, English, social studies, and science. Grade point average was used as an index of academic achievement in each subject area.   Intelligence was controlled.

The major findings were:

1.   General self-concept and academic performance were positively and significantly related (+.57 for males and +.57 for females); the relationship held even when I. Q. was controlled.

2.   There were specific self-concepts of ability related to specific areas of academic performance.   These specific self-concepts were found to be significantly better predictors of specific subject achievement than was general self-concept.

3.   General self-concept was positively and significantly related to the student's perception of how a few significant persons evaluated him.   His self-concepts in the various subjects were related to his perception of how a number of other persons evaluated him as a student.

The implications of changing self-concept are considered. The writers suggest that self-concept is a key factor in role performance and that changes in self-concept should result in changes in performance.

*   *   *   *

We view these findings as being important for several reasons. First, the possibility that self-concept may be changed should be noted. Second, if changes in self-concept may lead to changes in academic performance, then it is also possible that changes in academic performance may lead to changes in self-concept. The idea that there are general and specific self-concepts of ability suggests that we might change self-concept in specific subject areas by increasing a student's performance without necessarily first changing his general academic self-concept. Perhaps enough changes in his specific self-concepts would eventually lead to changes in his general self-concept. Finally, the study clearly shows that self-concept derives from the individual's perception of the evaluations that personally significant people make of him.

A, E

Carroll, John B. , 1963.
"Programed Instruction and Student Ability. "
Journal of Programed Instruction, 2, 7-11.

This paper attempts to account for the large individual differences in learning rate found under programed instruction. The results for two studies in foreign language learning are reported.

In the first, college students and adults (n = 14) were taught spoken Mandarin Chinese by means of a special audio-visual machine. The subjects worked for about an hour a day, three to five days a week. At the end of the sixth instructional loop, they were given an auditory comprehension test consisting of 25 sentences covering all previously taught vocabulary and grammar. In the second study, college students (n = 26) were taught the Arabic writing system. In both studies, the subjects' foreign language aptitude was measured by the Carroll-Sapon Modern Language Aptitude Test.

The first study's results indicate a strong relationship between the students' foreign language aptitude scores and both the level to which and the rate at which they learned. The correlation between MLAT total score and the auditory comprehension test score was +.60, and between the MLAT total score and time to finish the program, -.72. The correlation between time to finish and the comprehension test score was -.44. The second study's

findings indicate that when time allowed for learning was held relatively constant for all students, then their performance on the final
examination was more than ordinarily affected by differences in their
aptitudes.

*   *   *   *

These data suggest that aptitudes are predictive of both the
rate at which and the level to which students will learn.   Further,
they indicate that if time is held relatively constant, such that some
students are not allowed the time they need to learn, then individual
differences in aptitudes will play an unusually great role in student
achievement.

C, A, D, F

Carroll, J. B. , and Spearitt, D. , 1967.
A Study of a   Model of School Learning.
Monograph No. 4.   Cambridge, Massachusetts: Harvard University,
    Center for Research and Development of Educational Differ-
    ences.

A brief recapitulation of Carroll's "Model of School Learning"
and the results of an experimental study of some variables in the
model are presented. In particular, the influence of sex, intelligence, and quality of instruction on learning rates, learning efficiency, perseverance, and interest were examined in the study.
Two self-instructional booklets were prepared to teach some
rules about verbs of an artificial language. The booklets differed
only in their presentation of the rules and in the amount of explanation of mistakes. Form A, the high quality of instruction form,
presented each rule, tested it before presentation of the next rule,
and referred the student to pages on which his mistakes were fully
explained. Form B, the low quality of instruction form, presented
too much information at one time in a disorganized manner. The
explanations of mistakes were inadequate. These forms were
randomly assigned to a sample of sixth graders (n = 208) who had
been divided into three intelligence groups: high, above-average,
average to low. Measures of learning rate, level of achievement,
interest, and perseverance were taken.
The results were as follows:

1. Time to criterion
    Although not all subjects reached the predefined criterion
    score on either of the achievement measures, those who
    did required significantly less time on Form A than on
    Form B. Time to criterion was significantly related to

intelligence, but not sex. There was no interaction between intelligence and quality of instruction, suggesting
that poor quality of instruction affected high- as well as
low-intelligence students.

2. Perseverance (Time willing to spend)
There was an interaction between intelligence and the
quality of instruction with respect to the student's willingness to persevere on a difficult post-experimental task.
Students who used Form A in the main learning task spent
more time on the post-task if they were in the high or the
low, but not in the middle, intelligence group. The authors
speculate that the middle intelligence group applied themselves more to difficult, poorly presented material, while
those with high and low I. Q. 's tended to lose interest
quickly. Thus poor quality of instruction may decrease
perseverance for high- and low-intelligence students and
increase it for the average-intelligence students.

3. Learning Efficiency
Learning was inefficient when students had insufficient
opportunity (restricted time) to learn, particularly where
the instructional quality was poor and subjects were of
lower intelligence.

4. Interest
There was some tendency for the high-intelligence children and for those performing well on the criterion task to
express more interest in the task. On the whole, however,
interest was a negligible factor.

C

Coleman, James, et al. , 1966.
Equality of Educational Opportunity.
Final Report, USOE, Report No. 38001. Washington, D. C.:
United States National Center for Educational Statistics.

This study was a large-scale attempt to determine how far
American public schools have moved toward the ideal of providing
equal educational opportunities for all students. It examined some
of the critical factors related to student achievement and quality
education focusing particularly on factors affecting the education,
and hence achievement, of minority-group children. One portion of
the study dealt with the relationship between certain teacher characteristics and pupil achievement as measured by standardized achievement tests for grades 1, 3, 6, 9, and 12.

These data indicated that teacher quality was positively related to pupil achievement and that its influence was greater at the
higher grade levels. This finding seemed to indicate the cumulative
effect of teacher quality on student achievement. Teacher quality
was more highly related to the achievement of minority-group
children than to that of other children.

The teacher characteristics most highly related to pupil
achievement were educational background and especially verbal
ability. Teachers' verbal ability had its greatest effects on the
achievement of minority students, and these effects increased beginning especially with the sixth grade. This increase was taken to
indicate the cumulative effect of teacher quality over time.

*   *   *   *

We take these data to suggest a clear relationship between
quality of instruction (teacher's verbal ability) and pupil achievement. Also, they suggest that, in general, the quality of instruction is of greatest significance for groups of students at the lower
portion of the ability or achievement distribution.

G

Collins, Kenneth M. , 1969.
"A Strategy for Mastery Learning in Freshman Mathematics. "
Unpublished study, Purdue University, Division of Mathematical
    Sciences.

This study investigated the effectiveness of Bloom's mastery
learning strategy for the teaching of freshman college mathematics.
The research involved two modern algebra courses for liberal arts
majors (n = 50 approximately) and two calculus courses for engineering and science majors (n = 40 approximately).

These courses were broken into smaller units, and students
were assigned to learn the units under either mastery or non-mastery conditions. The mastery students were given a list of the
objectives to be covered in each unit, each class session, and each
assignment. During each session, they had five to ten minutes to
solve a problem based on the objectives covered in the preceding
session and assignment. Then, the problem was discussed and
questions answered. The non-mastery learners were given neither
a list of objectives nor daily problems. Both mastery and non-mastery students used the same textbook, received the same assignments, covered the same material in class, and took the same unit
tests. Grades were determined by averaging student scores on the
unit tests.

In the modern algebra classes, 75% of the mastery compared

to only 30% of the non-mastery students achieved the mastery criterion of an A or B grade. The calculus classes' results were similar: 65% of the mastery compared to 40% of the non-mastery students achieved the criterion. In both the modern algebra and the calculus courses, D and F grades were for all practical purposes eliminated for mastery students. The smaller difference in the percentages of students who attained the criterion under mastery and non-mastery learning conditions for the calculus courses may be attributed to three factors: a) the greater importance of the courses to all engineering and science students; b) the higher and more homogeneous mathematical ability of the calculus students; and c) the clearer relationship between the problems discussed in class and the unit test problems.

(K. M. C.)

G, C

Collins, Kenneth M. , 1970.
"A Strategy for Mastery Learning in Modern Mathematics. "
Unpublished study, Purdue University, Division of Mathematical
    Sciences.

This study investigated the effectiveness of the different variables in Bloom's mastery learning strategy for teaching modern mathematics at the junior high school level. The research used six classes (n = 25 each, approximately) drawn from a modern mathematics course for eighth graders. All the students were pretested for entering behavior and some of the course objectives. There were no differences between the classes on the pretests.

The course was broken into smaller units and a list of objectives for each unit was constructed. Each list indicated the objectives to be covered per class session and assignment. One class (Treatment 1) was given only the lists of objectives. A second class (Treatment 2) was given the lists plus a problem during each session testing the objectives covered in the previous session and assignment. After five to ten minutes to work on the problem, it was discussed and questions answered. Specific prescriptions were then provided for using the textbook, classnotes, and handouts to learn the objectives not mastered. The third class (Treatment 3) received the lists of objectives, the diagnostic problems, and the review prescriptions. In addition, they were provided alternative learning resources such as other textbooks, workbooks, games, and SRA instructional kits. The fourth class (Treatment 4) received only the problems and review prescriptions. The fifth class (Treatment 5) received only the problems. Finally, the control treatment (Treatment 6) received none of the preceding materials and relied on classwork and assignments only to learn the material. All classes were given the same unit tests based on the lists of objectives. Grades were determined by average student scores on the unit tests.

The results indicated major differences in the effects of the various treatments in helping students to learn to the mastery criterion of an A or B grade. Treatments 2 and 3 helped 80% of their students to achieve mastery. Treatments 4, 1, and 5 assisted 70%, 60%, and 50% respectively to achieve mastery. Further, treatments 1 through 4 practically eliminated D and F grades. These findings suggest, therefore, the great importance of specifying through our instructional and testing procedures the objectives students are expected to master. They also suggest the major effects that diagnostic testing can have on student achievement when coupled with a specific review prescription of what students can do to complete their learning. The diagnostic problems and review prescriptions were so effective here that the alternative learning resources were apparently superfluous.

(K. M. C.)

*   *   *   *

The study clearly indicates the cumulative effects on student achievement of the addition of the various mastery learning variables to the instruction. Suppose the per cent of students attaining mastery under control conditions (40%) is used as a base. The results suggest that the addition to the instruction of the unit objective lists increased the percentage of students attaining mastery from 40% to 60%. The addition of the diagnostic problems based upon these objectives appears to have augmented the percentage of students attaining mastery another 10% from 60% to approximately 70%. Finally, the addition of the specific review prescriptions based upon the diagnostic information hiked the percentage from 70% to 80%. Thus, the combined use of the objectives, diagnostic problems, and review prescriptions, systematically increased the per cent of students attaining mastery from 40% under control conditions to 80% under mastery conditions.

C, A

Cronbach, L. J. , and Snow, R. E. , 1969.
Individual Differences in Learning Ability as a Function of Instructional Variables.
Final Report, USOE, Contract No. OEC 4-6-061269-1217. Stanford, California: Stanford University, School of Education.

This is a careful and critical review of the literature relating to aptitude-treatment interaction (ATI) research. The review was supplemented by a series of experiments and data re-analyses carried out in connection with the project.

A major portion of the review is concerned with methodological issues in constructing ATI studies and analyzing the results. In sum, the authors find most previous studies to be inconclusive due to the way the problems were posed, the methods by which the data were analyzed, and their contradictory results. Few if any inter- actions in the literature are clearly confirmed.

A major part of the problem with previous studies is the fact that they have weakly conceptualized both the aptitude and the treat- ment dimensions. Cronbach and Snow hypothesize, for example, that to simply characterize aptitudes and treatments in such terms as "spatial" is unlikely to identify combinations of variables worth investigating. They also assert that treatments used in the past have suffered from brevity and artificiality.

While few interactions are found, the review does suggest possible directions for future research. First, the literature reviewed indicates that studies which employed narrowly defined aptitudes and those that employed varied programed instructional techniques usually failed to produce ATI's. However, there is much evidence to suggest that it might be possible to establish pairs of instructional treatments that interact with general ability. Gen- eral ability, conceived of as the ability to learn, was found to cor- relate with learning outcomes in both the classroom and controlled experimental conditions. We must understand how general ability enters into the learning activity of pupils and just what in this abil- ity complex is relevant at various points in the learning process.

One of the experiments, for example, attempted to relate measures of spatial orientation, visualization, and verbal compre- hension with instructional treatments that made varying use of a graphical-pictorial representation of ideas. No interactions were found. The pictorial treatment did not capitalize on the spatial talents of the subjects to a greater degree than the verbal treatment. These results led the authors to question the hypothesis that verbal ability necessarily facilitates the ability to learn verbal instruction or tasks, spatial ability to learn spatial tasks, and so on. A second investigation compared a structured, phonics treatment in beginning reading with more conventional "whole-word" reading instruction. The phonics instruction appeared to be best for low-ability children, while the whole-word treatment best served high-ability children.

*   *   *   *

This report is the most comprehensive investigation to date of the aptitude-instructional treatment interaction hypothesis. In general, it suggests that instructional treatments may be developed

to interact with student aptitudes and holds out hope that further
investigations will identify methods and modes of instruction which
can maximize learning for selected groups of learners.   Thus
improving the quality of instruction can optimize the learning for
particular learners.   Hopefully, curriculum makers and teachers
will eventually develop approaches to instruction which will best
serve the needs of different groups of learners.

C, B

Davis, John B., Jr., 1967.
"An Investigation of the Interaction of Certain Instructional Strate-
    gies with the Structure of Basic Mental Abilities in the Learn-
    ing of Some Mathematical Operations. "
Unpublished Ph.D. dissertation,   Florida State University.

    The relationship between instructional strategies, basic abil-
ities or aptitudes, and achievement in mathematics was examined.
It was hypothesized that performance in mathematics is the result
of the interaction between the forms in which the subject matter is
presented and the intellectual abilities possessed by the student.
    Two sets of materials dealing with the same mathematics
subject matter (computing derivatives and vector multiplication),
but differing in the aptitudes they required for optimal achievement,
were prepared. One set used symbolic content and the other, semantic content following distinctions made by Guilford. A reference
battery of various mental ability tests, drawn from Guilford's work,
and the two learning programs were administered to three different
samples. The first two samples consisted of college undergraduates.
The third sample was drawn from a group of tenth graders. In the
case of each sample, subjects were randomly assigned to one of
the two presentations of the subject matter (semantic or symbolic).
Achievement test scores covering the subject matter were also
obtained.
    For both college samples, but not for the high school group,
significant interactions were found between aptitude patterns of
students and the content form in which the mathematics was presented. Maximum achievement ocurred when the content form was
congruent with the individual's pattern of ability factors. For example, the correlation between total achievement test score and
measures of the mental ability cognition of semantic classes (CHC)
was +.73 for the semantic group and -.41 for the symbolic group.
The higher the person's score on the CHC test in the symbolic group,
the lower would be his predicted score on the achievement test.
Similarly, an interaction was found for the ability factor convergent
production of semantic implications (NMI). It seemed not to matter

whether a student was in the symbolic or the semantic group if his
NMI score was high, but if his score was low, a student in the
semantic group could be predicted to attain a higher achievement
score than one in the symbolic group. Finally, while both the
semantic and symbolic factor reference test scores were significant predictors of achievement on the semantic learning materials
posttest, only the symbolic factor tests were significant predictors
of achievement on the symbolic learning materials posttest.

*   *   *   *

We take these findings to indicate the following points. First,
the same content or subject matter may be taught in different forms.
The forms in which the subject matter is taught will give an advantage to students with aptitudes congruent with the mode of presentation, while it will place other students (low in these relevant aptitudes) at a disadvantage. Finally, the quality of instruction may
be thought of as the relevance of the particular form of instruction
(and instructional materials) to the particular aptitudes possessed
by students (individuals or groups).

F

Feather, N. T., 1966.
"Effects of Prior Success and Failure on Expectations of Success
    and Subsequent Performance. "
Journal of Personality and Social Psychology, 3, 287-98.

This experiment investigated the relationships between an
individual's orientation toward a task (seeking success or avoiding
failure), his expectation of the tasks at hand (easy or difficult), and
his initial experiences with the task (actual success or failure).
The entire theoretical framework for the experiment was derived
from a theory of achievement motivation.

The sample consisted of 72 college students. The subjects
worked at a task consisting of 15 anagrams. On the first five
anagrams, half of the subjects were given unsolvable anagrams so
that they failed (initial failure), and half were given very easy
anagrams so that they succeeded (initial success). Half of the
subjects were then told that the remaining anagrams would be easier
than most (high expectation) and half were told they would be more
difficult than most (low expectation). In reality, however, the last
ten anagrams were all of approximately 50 per cent difficulty.
Measures of need-achievement and test anxiety indicated the subject's general orientation toward any task (success versus failure
orientated). Finally, the subject's estimate of his probability of
success on each anagram was obtained before the anagram was given.

The results indicated the important influence of prior success or failure on the individual's expectations of later success and actual performance. Changes in expectations of success were greater following uniform initial failure than uniform success. Those who failed on the first five anagrams expected to continue to fail (i.e., gave low estimates of their probability to succeed). These subjects also performed significantly lower ($p < .01$) on the remaining anagrams than those who initially succeeded. The data also showed that in certain cases a person's general orientation toward a task (success or failure oriented) seemed to further exaggerate the influence of the initial success or failure condition on his expectations of success.

A, C

Gagné, R. M., and Paradise, N. E., 1961.
Abilities and Learning Sets in Knowledge Acquisition.
Psychological Monographs, 75, No. 14. (Whole Number 518.)

This paper examines some of the causes of individual differences in student performance on a learning program. It tests the hypothesis that learning rate is determined by different kinds and amounts of knowledge, hereafter referred to as intellectual skills, and examines the interrelationship between these skills, several basic abilities, and performance on a learning task.

A learning program in solving linear algebraic equations was analyzed into a learning hierarchy consisting of 1) a series of ordered intellectual skills and 2) the basic abilities upon which the simplest skills seemed to rest. A sample of 118 seventh graders was studied. Measures of the basic abilities relevant and irrelevant to the simplest skills were obtained prior to administering the learning program. Learning rate was measured by the number of skills attained during successive short intervals. Posttests yielded measures of achievement on each of the component skills and performance on a final equation solving task.

The findings indicated that the basic abilities were predictive of the learning rate of the skills to which they were logically relevant; however, the abilities were more highly related to learning rate for the simpler skills. The learning rate for the more-complex skills depended increasingly upon the acquisition of the preceding and related less-complex skills. Thus the conclusion was that basic abilities may be thought of as the most simple and general learning skills which support the learning of more complex skills by facilitating the learning of the related less-complex skills.

*   *   *   *

In our view, this study illustrates the following points. First, since learning hierarchies can be identified in advance and found in practice, the validity of the concept of learning hierarchies is established. Second, the finding that the acquistion of more-complex skills seems to rest on the learning of related less-complex components of the hierarchy suggests that mastery of a task can not be attained unless its less-complex skills are thoroughly learned. The possession of certain basic abilities (entry behaviors) should facilitate the learning of these skills. Finally, the fact that the learning rate for more-complex skills depends increasingly upon the attainment of relevant less-complex skills implies that if we can ensure that these less-complex skills are learned, we may be able to reduce the amount of time necessary to learn more-complex tasks. Hence we might be able to make all students' learning more efficient and reduce the great variation in the time students typically require to learn a task.

G

Gentile, J. Ronald, 1970.
"A Mastery Strategy for Introductory Educational Psychology."
Unpublished materials, State University of New York at Buffalo,
    Department of Educational Psychology.

These materials describe a mastery approach to the teaching of a course in introductory educational psychology. The strategy's main purposes were: a) to guarantee that all students mastered the course concepts, b) to demonstrate how instruction which emphasized cooperative rather than competitive learning could be organized in the classroom, and c) to maximize interactions among students, student proctors and the teacher.

In the approach used, student learning was self-paced over small instructional units. Study questions were provided for each unit delimiting the points to be mastered. Upon completion of each unit, the student scheduled an interview session with a classmate. At this session, he explained the material just learned in his own words. His classmate listened, asked questions about confusing points, and commented favorably on points explained clearly and fluently. Both learners then decided whether the speaker was ready for the unit mastery test. If so, a test was obtained from his proctor (a student who had previously mastered the material). The completed test was returned to the proctor for correction - - not grading - - followed by a discussion of unmastered material. If the proctor felt the student had mastered the unit, the pupil was allowed

to proceed to the next. Otherwise, he was asked to review and to
return for retesting. Proctors and the instructor were available
at all times to help pupils review. The student was cycled through
review and retesting until he attained mastery of the unit. Lectures
and demonstrations were scheduled only after a majority of students
had mastered enough material to make them worthwhile, and attendance was not compulsory. Each student who mastered all the units
received an A.

The approach produced striking cognitive and especially
affective results compared to a similar course (n = 52) more con-
ventionally taught through large required lectures and smaller
discussion group sessions. The mastery approach produced significantly better understanding (p < .001) of comparable material
taught in both courses. On identical forms of a course evaluation
sheet, 74% of the mastery students compared to only 21% of the
other students indicated they enjoyed taking the course. The mastery students rated the course as one of the best they had ever
taken and indicated they would highly recommend it to their friends.
Their favorable response to the strategy was attributed mostly to
the approach, the almost guaranteed "A", the responsiveness of
the proctors, and the availability of the instructor.

                                                            E, G
Glaser, Robert, 1968.
"Adapting the Elementary School Curriculum to Individual Perfor-
        mance. "
In Proceedings of the 1967 Invitational Conference on Testing Prob-
        lems. Princeton: Educational Testing Service, 3-36.

        This paper presents some of the theory behind the Individually
Prescribed Instruction (IPI) Project at Pittsburgh and data for the
first few years of the program. IPI is designed to achieve individualized instruction in grades K through 6 in the subject areas of
reading, science, and arithmetic. By means of detailed sequences
of objectives in each area, the preparation of self-study materials
keyed to each objective, and procedures for testing and individualized lesson planning, each student progresses through the curriculum at his own pace. A major portion of the student's class time
is spent in work designed for him on the basis of his level of prior
achievement and other factors. An achievement level criterion of
85 per cent must be reached on each learning unit before the student moves on to the next.

The data concern various measures of rate of learning in the
mathematics curriculum. They indicate wide individual differences
in the number of units reached and the number mastered to the

criterion level over time. The average time taken to master a
unit was 12 days, with a range of one to 60 days. The data for 100
students who had been in the program for three years indicate
that during this time the faster students mastered almost five times
as many units as the slower students. The data also indicate an
increasing relationship between number of units covered and year
in program. Finally, the amount of knowledge that the student had
at the beginning of his first year in the program was highly related
to the number of units covered over a three year period (+. 72).

* * * *

The research so far does demonstrate that students can
achieve mastery over each unit of learning, although there is considerable variation in the length of time required to achieve it.
Further research is being done on the relationship between individual differences and instructional methods.

G

Green, Ben A. , Jr. , 1969.
A Self-Paced Course in Freshman Physics.
Cambridge, Massachusetts: Massachusetts Institute of Technology,
    Education Research Center.

This paper describes an effective, inexpensive mastery learning approach to the teaching of introductory physics. The aim of
the strategy was to produce a "personalized" course in which students could work independently of their classmates at times and
places of their own choosing, yet interact face-to-face with student
tutors to obtain help and to check on their learning progress.
The learning was self-paced over small instructional units
prepared by the teacher. Each unit consisted of an introduction, a
presentation of the major objectives to be mastered, suggested
study procedures (e.g., reading assignments in the course textbook),
and a series of study questions. Upon completion of each unit, students took a short, written, ungraded mastery test covering the unit
objectives. The tests emphasized comprehension rather than memory and were designed to pace student learning. Student tutors corrected these tests and helped students overcome their learning difficulties. For especially difficult units, programed review materials were used. Each student had to demonstrate mastery on a
unit before proceeding to the next. Lectures and demonstrations
were given by the instructor only when a sufficient number of students had mastered the prerequisite material. These sessions
were aimed at stimulating learning rather than transmitting material to be learned.

The results for 150 undergraduates are briefly described.
Students enjoyed the course and performed as well on a final examination as students learning under the traditional lecture-discussion-
demonstration approach. The mastery approach's success is attributed to the use of student tutors, who added a very valuable
personal-social dimension to the course, and to the sparse use of
the tools of educational technology (e.g., filmstrips, tapes). The
technological gadgets did not work as well as the tutors and, in
fact, diverted student attention from learning. The course has
subsequently been expanded.

                                                                    G

Keller, Fred S., 1968.
"Goodbye, Teacher . . ."
Journal of Applied Behavior Analysis, 1, 79-89.

        This paper summarizes the author's experience with an inex-
pensive and effective mastery learning strategy in which the teacher
plays the very new role of an educational engineer or contingency
manager responsible for facilitating the learning of all students.
The strategy, developed to teach general psychology, used the
principles of reinforcement theory. Student proctors provided the
necessary types and amounts of reinforcement.
        The approach used short, teacher prepared study units through
which students could proceed at their own pace. Each unit indicated
the objectives the student was expected to master and suggested
specific study procedures. At the end of each unit, students asked
their proctor (a student who had already completed the course) for
a short, ungraded essay test covering the unit's objectives. If the
student exhibited mastery on each objective, the proctor commended
his performance and allowed him to proceed to the next learning
unit. If the student did not exhibit mastery of the unit, the proctor
briefly tutored him on the unmastered material and then asked him
to review before returning for retesting. The use of proctors
allowed repeated testing, immediate feedback of results, and tutoring and, in general, created a highly personal-social learning at-
mosphere. Lectures and demonstrations by the teacher were
scheduled only after a sufficient number of students had mastered
enough material to make them worthwhile. Final grades were
determined by performance on a teacher prepared final examination,
laboratory work, and the number of learning units completed.
        The results for several classes taught in this way by both the
author and his colleagues are reported. The results for two courses
(n = 200 per course, approximately) taught one year apart under the
strategy were almost identical - - 65% to 70% of the students

received A's or B's. Each time the strategy was applied, it produced a large percentage of A's and B's, but few D's and F's.

The article closes by reflecting on the program's unique features. It is suggested that the mastery strategy is superior to any
programed method of individualizing instruction because it provides
a very important personal-social interactional component. The
author calls for teachers to assume more responsibility for their
students' learning and to manage student learning more efficiently.

G

Kersh, Mildred E., 1970.
"A Strategy for Mastery Learning in Fifth-Grade Arithmetic."
Unpublished Ph.D. dissertation, University of Chicago.

This study investigated the effectiveness of a strategy based
on John Carroll's "Model of School Learning" to increase the proportion of students attaining mastery (grade of A or B) in one year
in fifth-grade arithmetic. The strategy attempted to encourage the
pupil to maintain mastery throughout his learning.

The activities in this strategy were divided into four phases.
In the first phase, the teacher conducted the arithmetic class in
his usual style for three to four weeks. When the unit was completed, a diagnostic test based on the objectives of instruction was
administered. On the basis of his test errors, the student was
directed to alternative learning resources. After a week's opportunity to use these resources, a retest was administered. This
retest provided positive reinforcement to students who had used
the alternative resources to correct their errors. The sample
included students from six fifth-grade classes from a socio-eco-
nomically disadvantaged population and six fifth-grade classes
from an advantaged population.

The results indicated that on the same achievement test and
using the same mastery standard, there were significant increases
in the proportion of experimental students (mastery class) attaining mastery compared to the proportion of the teacher's students
from the previous year (control class) attaining mastery. These
increases ranged for one advantaged class from 19% mastery in the
1966 control class to 75% mastery in the same teacher's 1967 mastery learning class. Moreover, a disadvantaged class increased
from 0% attaining mastery in 1966 to 20% attaining it in the 1967
mastery learning class. Note, in these examples, that the disadvantaged mastery class performed as well as an advantaged control
class. Perhaps the strategy might be helpful in at least partially
overcoming the cumulative deficit in learning manifested by socio-
economically disadvantaged students.

(M.E.K.)

Kim, Hogwon, 1968.
"Learning Rates, Aptitudes, and Achievements. "
Unpublished Ph. D. dissertation, University of Chicago.

This paper investigates the relation between aptitudes and
both learning rates and achievement levels. Two hypotheses were
of special interest: 1) that learning rate can be predicted by relevant aptitudes; and 2) that different aptitudes must be used to predict learning rates on different learning tasks.

Learning tasks involving beginning German, simple statistics,
and logical reasoning were taught to mastery levels for samples of
about 50 fifth and sixth graders. For each learning task, the learning rates and levels of achievement at several time periods in the
learning were correlated to their Primary Mental Abilities Test
and their Otis Quick Scoring Mental Ability Test scores.

Measures of final achievement correlated highly with measures
of achievement at the end of each time period (the correlations
were typically above +. 75), suggesting that learning rates and
achievement levels were interchangeable in this type of learning
situation. Measures of verbal ability and general intelligence gave
moderate correlations (about +.40) with learning rates in each of
the learning tasks, suggesting that ability to understand instruction
affects learning rate. Particular aptitudes were related to learning
rate for each task. Memory best predicted learning rate for
German words. Reasoning and Number Facility best predicted
learning rate for statistical concepts and operations. Spatial Relations best predicted learning rate for logical syllogisms.

(B. S. B.)

*   *   *   *

The connection between the spatial relations aptitude test and
rate of learning logical reasoning is of special interest to the editor.
It is believed this correlation was high because Venn diagrams
were used in the learning task. The student had to translate the
logical syllogisms into spatial forms in order to solve the problems.
Logical reasoning could probably be taught by other methods emphasizing other aptitudes (e. g. , verbal, numerical, memory, or
reasoning ability). It is hoped that further work can be done along
these lines to further demonstrate interactions between aptitude
and instructional method.

Kim, Hogwon, et al. , 1969.
A Study of the Bloom Strategies for Mastery Learning.
Seoul: Korean Institute for Research in the Behavioral Sciences.
   (In Korean)

This study examines the effectiveness of Bloom's strategies for mastery learning in Korea where classes are predominantly very large (usually one teacher to 70 students).

The research sample consisted of 272 seventh graders. Half were assigned to the mastery learning (experimental) group and half to the non-mastery learning (control) group. These groups were comparable in terms of I.Q. and prior mathematics achievement. Both groups were taught a unit on simple geometric figures for eight sessions by their own teachers. The instructional procedures followed for both control and mastery students included:

a) Clarification for students of the objectives to be mastered.

b) Regular instructional periods in which an efficient use of teaching and learning time was emphasized, such as the use of charts and audio-visual material in place of time-consuming blackboard writing.

c) A final summative achievement test.

In addition, for only the mastery students the following procedures were followed:

d) Formative tests given to students as soon as they completed the sub-unit learning tasks. Three ten-minute tests were administered as part of the regular instruction and scored by the students.

e) Remedial programed instruction for students who scored less than 80% on each formative test. Each unit program consisted of about 40 to 50 frames and was studied individually as homework.

f) Review questions provided for each child. Some of these questions were used for instructional purposes in the regular classroom sessions and some were used in small-group cooperative study sessions. Students who completed the learning early were encouraged to help those who had scored poorly on the formative tests.

The results indicate that 74% of the experimental compared to only 40% of the control students attained the mastery criterion of at least 80 per cent correct answers on the summative achievement test. The data also reveal an interesting relationship between I.Q.

and achievement under the mastery and non-mastery learning conditions. Of those with below-average I.Q. (< 93), 50% of the experimental students compared to only 8% of the control students achieved the mastery criterion. Of those with above-average I.Q., 95% of the experimental students reached the criterion compared to only 64% of the control students. Thus, almost as many mastery students with below-average I.Q. as control students with above-average I.Q. reached the criterion. Mastery learning was most effective for students with below-average I.Q.

*   *   *   *

The editor interprets these findings to suggest the powerful effect feedback/correction procedures can have on each student's learning when used to supplement their original instruction under such difficult instructional conditions as 70 students to one teacher. Further, these results suggest that feedback/correction procedures may be able to offset the strong effects that I.Q. usually has on student achievement under typical classroom instruction. If this is true, then Kim's results raise doubts about the role that I.Q. need play in student learning.

G

Kim, Hogwon, et al. , 1970.
The Mastery Learning Project in the Middle Schools.
Seoul: Korean Institute for Research in the Behavioral Sciences.
    (In Korean.)

This study reports the results of a large-scale expansion of the earlier experiment on mastery learning. Nine middle schools (approximately 5,800 seventh graders) in Seoul participated. The experiment covered eight weeks of learning in mathematics and English.
Instructional strategies adopted in this project were much the same as those used in the first study (Kim, et al. , 1969), except that a diagnostic test of learning deficiencies and the necessary compensatory programed units were administered prior to the regular instructional , experimental sessions. Because of the greater scale of this project compared to the earlier experiment, it was found useful to prepare a flow chart for purposes of designing the instruction. This chart was as follows:

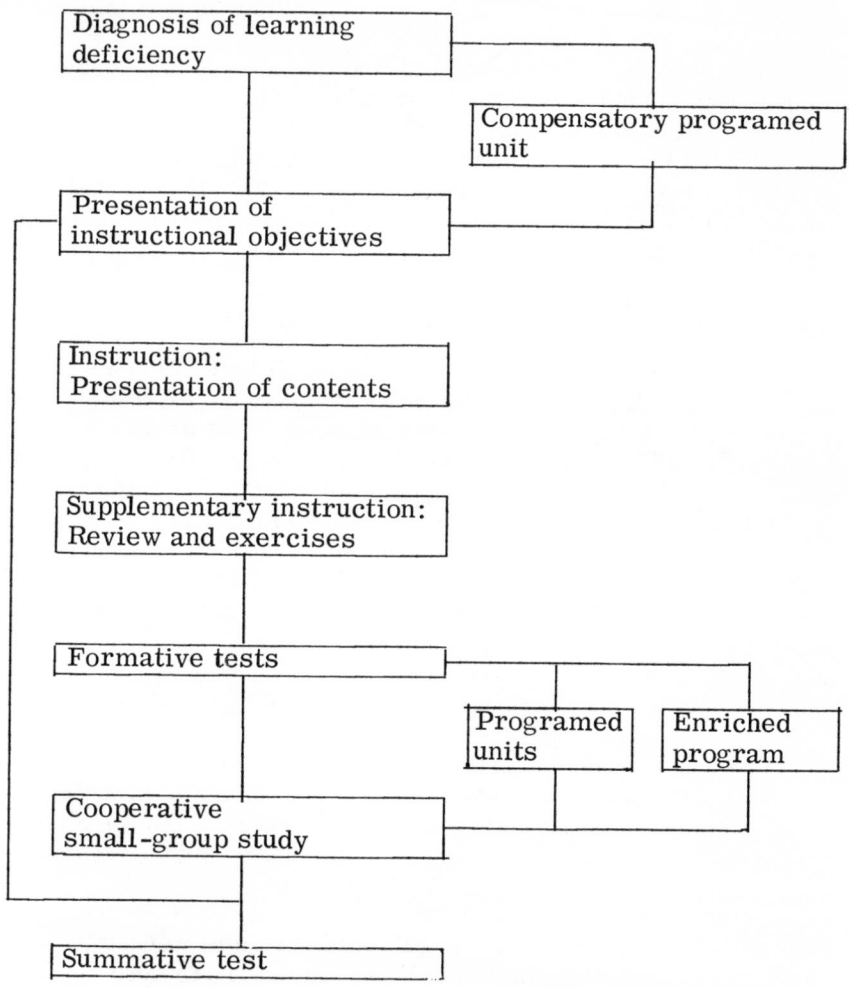

In the current project, enriched programs have not been included, but they are planned for the next project.

The results indicate that the percentage of experimental students attaining mastery (80 per cent correct scores on final summative examinations) varied widely across the sample schools. On the average , however, 72% of the students reached the mastery criterion by learning English under experimental conditions compared to only 28% learning under ordinary instructional conditions. In mathematics, an average of 61% of the mastery compared to 39% of the non-mastery students attained the summative achievement test criterion. Two schools did not follow the prescribed procedures. If the results for these schools are ignored, then 75% of the mastery students attained the criterion level in English and 67% in mathematics.

Fluctuations from school to school in the percentage of experimental students attaining the mastery criterion appear to have been caused by a) variation in the schools' learning climate, b) variation in the schools' and teachers' cooperation, c) inefficient utilization and administration of the instructional materials, and d) the failure of some teachers to follow the experimental operating procedures.

(H.K.)

*   *   *   *

The Korean Institute is systematically pursuing a long term research and development program in mastery learning. It began with a study of about 270 seventh graders in an experimental subject (geometric figures). The results were analyzed and the procedures improved. The program then went to nine schools, almost 6,000 seventh graders and two subjects (arithmetic and English as a second language). Again, the results were analyzed and the procedures improved. The present project involves 32,000 students with plans for expansion in the near future to about 50,000 students.

G

Mayo, Samuel T., Hunt, Ruth C., and Tremmel, Fred, 1968.
"A Mastery Approach to the Evaluation of Learning Statistics."
Paper presented at annual meeting of National Council on Measurement in Education, Chicago, Illinois.

A six-week summer session in introductory, university level statistics emphasized the use of homework and weekly formative tests accompanied by individual and small-group help as needed. Students were informed that their final grades would be determined by their performance rather than by their relative standing in the group.

On a previously used final examination in 1966, 65% of the mastery learning students (n = 17) received a grade of A in contrast with 3% of the 1966 comparison group. For final grades (based on mid-term and final examinations), 65% of the mastery group received A's in contrast to 5% of the comparison group.

In the tutoring sessions, it became evident that attitudes about mathematics and statistics were of central concern. The feedback evidence provided by the formative tests was especially useful as a basis for helping students in individual and group sessions.

(B.S.B.)

E, C

Merrill, M. David, Barton, Keith, and Wood, Larry E. , 1970.
"Specific Review in Learning a Hierarchical Imaginary Science. "
Journal of Educational Psychology, 61, 102-9.

This research examined the effectiveness of a procedure to
facilitate student learning of a hierarchical (sequential) learning
task. It was proposed that specific review at each stage where
difficulties were encountered in the task's learning should facilitate
learning at subsequent stages and produce greater end-of-task
achievement, transfer, and retention.

Forty college students were randomly assigned to two groups
to learn an imaginary science through a five-lesson teaching machine course. In the experimental group, a specific review procedure was used when the learner encountered difficulties. The
procedure consisted of a step-by-step explanation of the misunder-
stood material. The control group did not receive specific review.
In both groups, each lesson was followed by a quiz with no feedback
of results. Immediately following the five lessons and quizzes,
each subject was given form A or B of a criterion test. Three
weeks later, each subject retook either the same form of the criterion test, to measure retention, or the other form, to measure
transfer.

Of special interest for mastery learning, the findings indicate
that specific review following difficulties made experimental students' learning increasingly efficient. The total time spent on
original (not review) learning by the experimental group decreased
successively across the five lessons (p < .05). Further, the
total time spent by the experimental groups to complete the five
lessons and accompanying quizzes , even including the specific
review material, was slightly less than the time spent by the control group. In other words, the experimental students were presented more material than the control group, but they still learned
this material in less total time.

(R. W.)

*　　　*　　　*　　　*

This study is a replication of an earlier one (Merrill, 1965)
in which general rather than specific review was used. The earlier
study's findings suggested that a general review procedure actually
made student learning increasingly inefficient. The present study
suggests the need for specific rather than general correction/review
procedures for mastery learning strategies dealing with hierarchically or sequentially structured learning tasks. More time than
usual may have to be set aside early in the task's learning for
correction/review, but the time spent here should pay off in terms

of spending less learning time than usual later. Merrill's findings suggest that mastery at each stage in the student's learning can be maintained through specific correction/review procedures without using any more, and perhaps even less, instructional time than would ordinarily be spent.

F

Modu, Christopher C., 1969.
"Affective Consequences of Cognitive Changes."
Unpublished Ph.D. dissertation, University of Chicago.

The purpose of the investigation was to explore the extent to which perceived changes in cognitive achievement influence certain affective characteristics of college students. It was hypothesized that subjective feelings of success or failure produce personality changes in students and provide specific cues for positive or negative self-evaluation.

The discrepancies in grade averages between high school and college provided an operational basis for estimating students' perceptions of changes in their cognitive achievement and for classifying students by extent of change. Changes in a number of affective variables (namely, self-rating, level of aspiration, life-goals, interpersonal competency, leadership achievement, scientific, literary, art, speech-drama, and music achievements) over a one-year period were related to the grade discrepancies using longitudinal survey data of 2,433 students from 16 colleges and universities.

The grade discrepancies were found to be significantly related to changes in particular affective qualities. Both the direction and the magnitude of affective changes were positively related to the direction and magnitude of the grade discrepancies. Students ranged on an affective change continuum from negative to positive according to whether their grade averages deteriorated, remained stable, or improved. This relationship held across sex and persisted even when differences in academic aptitude and students' dissatisfaction with their college choice was controlled.

Of the affective variables, changes in self-rating and leadership qualities were found to be most noticeable, thus emphasizing the importance of self-esteem as a sensitive barometer of perceived cognitive changes in college students. Being responsive to subjective feelings of academic success or failure, self-esteem could be changed even in late adolescence by an appropriate manipulation of cognitive achievement. Changes in interest were found to be more closely associated with cognitive changes in areas related to students' major fields of study.

These findings indicate the need to reexamine prevalent grading practices and to ask what effects a particular mark has on the student's self-evaluation. They further suggest that learning strategies which promote higher levels of achievement and changes in grading procedures may prevent losses in a student's self-esteem, thus helping to prevent severe emotional disturbance among college students.

(C.M.)

G

Moore, J. W., Mahan, J. M., and Ritts, C. A., 1968.
"An Evaluation of the Continuous Progress Concept of Instruction with University Students."
Paper presented at the annual meeting of the American Educational Research Association, Chicago, Illinois.

Three courses - - biology, psychology, and philosophy - - were taught by instructional materials the student could use on his own. Students were tested as soon as they had completed each unit, and if they had not achieved mastery on the unit, they were directed to additional instructional materials and additional unit tests until they achieved mastery. The students were informed that they were expected to reach a predetermined achievement level which was equivalent to an A or B in the traditional grading system.

In biology and psychology, the students were matched on aptitude scores and randomly assigned to either the experimental or the control group course, with 35 students in each group. On the final examinations given both groups, the experimental (continuous progress) group was approximately one-half standard deviation above the control group.

In philosophy, the grades of the experimental group were compared to those of a comparison group from a previous year. Approximately four-fifths of the experimental group received an A or a B, compared to three-fifths of the comparison group.

The authors believe that the effectiveness of the continuous progress program cannot be attributed to any single variable. For some students it was the self-pacing and independent study, for others the emphasis on learning as opposed to working for marks, and for still others it may have been the mastery requirement or some combination of these factors.

(B.S.B.)

Payne, Margaret, 1963.
"The Use of Data in Curricular Decisions. "
Unpublished Ph. D. dissertation, University of Chicago.

A longitudinal study was made of arithmetic achievement as
measured by standardized achievement tests from grades 1 to 6.
In addition to the achievement measures in arithmetic, general
intelligence test scores, reading scores, and data on socio-economic variables were also obtained. The primary purpose of the
study was to determine how early a student's sixth-grade achievement (satisfactory or unsatisfactory) could be predicted as a basis
for making curricular and instructional decisions about him. Put
in other terms the study was an attempt to determine how much
time could be made available to the school to alter predicted
(unsatisfactory) levels of achievement. The study was made on
two groups of students (n = 74 and n = 106) for purposes of cross-
validation.

Sixth-grade achievement on the Metropolitan Achievement
Test was predicted with a multiple correlation of +. 68 by the middle
of the first grade and with a multiple correlation as high as +. 89
by the middle of the second grade. There was little improvement
in accuracy of prediction beyond the third grade.

(B. S. B.)

*   *   *   *

The editor regards this study as further evidence of the
consistency of achievement patterns over four or more years.
Sixth-grade achievement is highly predictable four or more years
earlier. Thus some students can clearly be identified as consistently doing well in school year after year, while other students
can be clearly identified as consistently doing poorly. Mastery
learning procedures are needed very early in the school careers
of pupils if they are to have a series of successful and rewarding
experiences from one school grade to another.

                                                        G
Postlewait, Samuel N. , Novak, Joseph D. , and Murray, Hal, 1964.
An Integrated Experience Approach to Learning with Emphasis on
        Independent Study.
Minneapolis: Burgess Publishing Company.

This curriculum effort was prompted by the view that students
now entering college possess a diversity of interests, backgrounds,
and capabilities. To accommodate student diversity, it was

proposed that teaching should include: 1) a variety of techniques including the use of media, 2) self-paced learning, and 3) increased student contact with teaching personnel to improve motivation. To test this idea, an experimental curriculum in freshman botany was developed.

In this curriculum, great emphasis was placed upon "independent study sessions" in which students proceeded at their own pace through course assignments making extensive use of tapes and films (3 hours per week). Small group discussions (1 hour per week) were used primarily for recitation and the discussion of problems or small research projects. Large group sessions (1 hour per week) were used to integrate and elucidate material and to assign homework and individual research projects. The teaching staff for up to 480 students included two full-time instructors, eight half-time teaching assistants, and two undergraduate assistants. Teaching assistants gave oral quizzes, discussed major concepts, and helped students complete especially difficult assignments.

Grades were based on the percentage of points earned out of a fixed total number of points possible. Points were accumulated through weekly quizzes - - a oral quiz taken each week when the student felt he had mastered the assignment and a written quiz taken in the small group sessions - - and through a comprehensive and a final practical examination.

No rigorous evaluation of the approach has been attempted. When compared with a conventional course taught by the senior author for over a decade, however, the new course seems to have helped more students reach higher achievement levels, considerably improved students' attitudes toward the course and made it possible to teach one-third more material per semester. Limited data also suggest that the course may have increased student transfer and retention. The grade distributions obtained under the program for four semesters were reported. The program seems to have become increasingly effective. During the first semester, 43% of the students received A or B grades, and 27% D's and F's. By the fourth semester, 64% received A's and B's and only 13% D's and F's. The fourth semester's results are strikingly different than the results obtained under a conventional system.

(R.W.)

F

Sears, Pauline S. , 1940.
"Levels of Aspiration in Academically Successful and Unsuccess-
    ful Children. "
Journal of Abnormal Social Psychology, 35, 498-536.

The hypothesis of this study is that a person's aspiration
pattern for a given task is determined in part by his past experiences of success or failure with perceptually similar tasks.

A student's past experience of success or failure was evaluated on the basis of his reading and arithmetic achievement in
grades 4, 5, and 6. Tasks used to measure level of aspiration
were derived from reading (multiple-choice word-meaning items)
and arithmetic (problems in addition). Three groups (n = 12 each)
were matched on age (mental and chronological) and sex and were
designated as follows: a "success" group (those previously successful in both reading and arithmetic), a "failure" group (those
low in reading and arithmetic) and a "differential" group (those
successful in reading but low in arithmetic). The tasks were
administered to the sample as speed tests. The subject was first
told his performance time and was subsequently asked for his level
of aspiration (estimated time) on the next task. A series of 20
tasks was presented to each subject. A discrepancy score was
calculated equal to the difference between his actual performance
time and his expected time.

The "failure" group when compared with the "success" group
showed larger discrepancy scores and greater variability in discrepancy scores. The "differential" group showed low discrepancy scores on reading but larger scores on arithmetic; these
results resembled those of the "success" group on reading and
those of the "failure" group on arithmetic. Differences between
the "differential" and the "success" groups in reading and between
the "differential" and "failure" groups in arithmetic were small.
The results are consistent with the hypothesis that experiences of
success and failure influence levels of aspiration.

D

Seashore, H. B.,and Bavelas, A. , 1942.
" A Study of Frustration in Children. "
Journal of Genetic Psychology, 61, 279-314.

The principle purposes of this study were to explore methods
of studying frustration in children and to observe the reactions of
a known group of children to a situation presumed to be frustrating.

Eighteen children were individually asked to "Draw a Man. "

After finishing a drawing the subjects were told, "Draw another man, this time a better one. " If a subject balked at drawing another man, he was asked by the experimenter to attempt one final drawing. When the "final" drawing was finished, the experimenter simply returned to his earlier request. The absence of any positive response to the children's efforts was considered by the authors to be a frustrating experience.

Two interesting results were reported: (1) there was a general tendency toward cognitive regression as measured in terms of changes in mental age as measured by the Goodenough scale; and (2) there was a general tendency to spend less and less time on each drawing. This decrease was not due to increased efficiency, but is interpreted here as a reaction to frustration.

We feel that the importance of this study lies in the positive relationship it suggests between persistence at a task and some form of external reinforcement. We suspect that this relationship may be especially important when there are objective criteria of success (e.g. , grades) which the subject is able to perceive as indications of his success or failure, or when the source of the external reinforcement is someone of importance to the subject (e.g. , a child's mother).

(W. J. W.)

G

Sherman, J. G. , 1967.
"Application of Reinforcement Principles to a College Course. "
Paper presented at the annual meeting of the American Educational
    Research Association, New York.

This paper reports on a mastery strategy for teaching introductory undergraduate psychology at Arizona State University. The strategy's objective was to provide individualized instruction and attention within the framework of mass education.

Learning in the approach used was self-paced over small instructional units, with assignment sheets prepared by the teacher as study guides. These sheets contained selections to be read from the textbook, hints on certain terms or data requiring special attention, a series of study questions, and some comments relating one unit to the next or bringing certain issues up to date. When a student completed a unit, he requested a unit readiness or mastery test from his proctor (a student who had already mastered the materials). The tests were ungraded and were designed to indicate any material in the unit the student had not mastered. If a student's test was perfect, he was allowed to proceed to the next unit. If not, he was asked to review and return for retesting. Proctors were always available for consultation. The student could not proceed until he had demonstrated perfect unit mastery. Unrequired lectures and demonstrations were given only when a sufficient number of students has mastered enough material to appreciate them. Final grades were based on the total number of units finished (50%), lab work (25%), and final examination performance (25%).

The strategy had strong cognitive and affective consequences. The normal grading curve disappeared: 50% of the students received A's and B's, and none received D's or F's. A substantial percentage of the students (39%), however, did not complete their learning until the following semester. Students exhibited positive attitudes toward the course, and nearly everyone who finished it wanted to become a proctor. Initially, however, students did resent the perfect per unit mastery requirement.

The strategy's success is attributed to two major factors. First, it contained all the advantages of a programed instruction course (e.g., immediate feedback, reinforcement, individual monitoring at every stage) but used all the traditional tools of the classroom - - textbook readings, lectures, demonstrations, discussion, and testing. Second, the use of student proctors provided an important kind of social reinforcement which is not typical of programed instruction.

C, G

Silberman, H., and Coulson, J., 1964.
Final report: Use of Exploratory Research and Individual Tutoring
    Techniques for the Development of Programing Methods and
    Theory.
Santa Monica, California: System Development Corporation.

The first part of this paper reports on the use of an exploratory tutorial approach for evaluation and revision of instructional programs. Programs representing both verbal and quantitative skills - - high-school geometry, junior-high-school Spanish, and first-grade reading and arithmetic - - were intensively studied. For each program, one experimenter served as the tutor while presenting the program to each student. Whenever the student encountered difficulties, tutorial assistance was provided. Records of student difficulties and the tutorial operations that overcame them were kept. Operations which overcame common problems were added to the program. Each revision was tested and analyzed, and after several such iterative revisions the final revised program was experimentally compared with the original program. In each case, mean student achievement was significantly greater for students using the revised program.

From the exploratory research some observations and principles were drawn. One important observation was the brighter
students tended to be less affected by deficient programs than less
intelligent students. They tended to compensate for the program's
failings and learned almost irrespective of program techniques.
The following principles were drawn. First, every program should
include items that cover every skill required in any criterion task
and every sub-skill prerequisite to the performance of these criterion skills (Gap principle). Second, the program should have no
unnecessary items (Irrelevancy principle). Third, students should
master each component skill before being allowed to advance to
more complex skills (Mastery principle). This could be accomplished by either permitting the student to move at his own rate
through the program or by providing alternative amounts of practice and/or alternative sequences of items contingent upon the student's performance. The three principles were shown to be consistent with a number of different conceptual models in learning.

The second portion of the paper describes an attempt to
experimentally verify these principles using a new sample and
program in logic.

E, A

Sjogren, Douglas D. , 1967.
"Achievement as a Function of Study Time. "
American Educational Research Journal, 4, 337-44.

In this study a basic proposition of the Carroll model was
examined, namely, that the degree of learning is a function of the
ratio of the time spent to the time needed to learn. The sample of
208 adults learned each of three different learning programs. The
subjects were randomly assigned so that each subject might learn
each program under a different time condition. Two of these conditions (A and B) allowed the subject to proceed at or near his
own rate, but the third condition (C) gave the subject a fixed
amount of time to learn. In the C condition the time allowed for
each frame of the program was the median amount of time that had
been taken by a different sample of adults.

For each subject studying a program in the C condition, it
was possible to derive a mean estimate of the time he needed to
learn the program from the time he had taken under the A and B
conditions. The time spent per program under the C condition
was fixed and approximately constant for each subject. The ratio
of the time spent to the time needed was then calculated and related
to scores on achievement tests over the program studied in the C
condition and to scores on an aptitude measure.

The results supported the Carroll model. There was a significant positive relationship between the ratio of time spent to the
time needed and the learning measures - - the achievement tests
and the aptitude scores. In addition, a measure of general intelligence was found to be highly related to the ratio (r = +.50 to +.60).
From this, the author hypothesizes that the ratio of time needed to
time spent might be the equivalent of an aptitude measure.

*   *   *   *

The editor interprets this study as indicating a significant
relationship between variation in time needed to complete a learning
task (since time spent was fixed) and both general intelligence and
achievement measures.

E. F

Smith, Henry L., and Eaton, Merrill T., 1939.
"The Relation of Retention to Speed of Learning."
Bulletin of the School of Education, Indiana University, 15, No. 3.

This article presents an in-depth study of the relationship of
retention to speed of learning. This relationship was examined
using six different types of learning materials - - nonsense
syllables, words, names and dates, geometric figures, symbols,
and poetry - - in each of three different degrees or conditions of
learning - - partial learning, complete learning, and over learning.
The sample consisted of 24 college freshmen of varying academic
abilities. Retention was measured by both the efficiency of recall
and the speed of relearning.

The central finding was that retention is independent of original learning speed. Also of interest, however, are some data that
show each subject's learning rate, relative to other students, on
the different types of learning materials and under the different
learning conditions. Despite the fact that the learning task was
essentially the same for each type of material - - that is, simply
memorization of a sequence - - the data indicate quite marked
variation in the speed with which individuals learned the different
materials. The editor has calculated some approximate rank
difference correlations between the speeds with which the subjects
learned the different types of material, In the complete learning
condition, the correlation between speed of learning the geometric
shapes versus the symbols was +.30. The correlations between
the speed of learning the poetry materials and the symbolic or
geometric shapes were +.52 and +.49 respectively. Thus an
individual who learns one type of material quickly will not necessarily learn other materials just as quickly.

*   *   *   *

This study's findings suggest that the rate at which a student learns does not affect his retention of the material he has learned. Also, they suggest that the student's rate of learning will vary for different types of tasks.

F

Stringer, L. A., and Glidewell, J. C., 1967.
Early Detection of Emotional Illnesses in School Children.
Final Report. St. Louis, Missouri: St. Louis County Health
   Department, Division of Research and Development.

This is a longitudinal study of the relationship between the academic progress of elementary school pupils and emotional illness. It is especially concerned with the interaction between deviant academic progress and emotional disturbance.

The academic progress of each pupil was plotted over a number of years. Pairs of children were selected who were from the same classroom, of the same sex, and of about the same age and I.Q., but who had markedly different academic progress patterns. Over a three-year period, social case workers held annual interviews with the mothers of these children to secure information about the child's history and his social-emotional characteristics and symptomatology, as well as an overall judgment of his mental health status. The total sample included 247 children drawn from grades 2 to 6. The final sample, with complete data for all three years, was 148.

Significant relationships were found between the overall estimate of mental health and the academic progress of the pupils. Two-thirds or more of the seriously disturbed children were identified correctly by the pattern of academic progress. A rating of the child's self-esteem was highly correlated with the number of mental health symptoms reported (+. 68), with his overall mental health rating (+. 82), and with his academic progress (+. 24). His mental health status correlated about +. 27 with his academic progress. Academic progress patterns were also found to be remarkably stable over the three-year period.

The writers conclude that consistent success in school over a number of years constitutes a type of immunization against mental illness, whereas consistent failure makes a child vulnerable to mental illness.

(B. S. B.)

G

Thompson, R. B. , 1941.
"Diagnosis and Remedial Instruction in Mathematics. "
School Science and Mathematics, 41, 125-28.

The results of a series of longitudinal studies carried out over a four-year period in the learning of arithmetic and algebra are reported. The studies were made in an effort to formulate a plan of instruction by which each student could progress at his own optimum rate of speed.

In general, a matched experimental versus control group design was used. In the experimental group, each student worked alone. Prior to beginning the study of any phase of the arithmetic or algebra, the student was given a diagnostic pretest to determine whether he had or had not previously mastered the material to be covered. If the student had mastered the material, he was given a pretest covering the next phase of instruction. This process was continued until weaknesses were found in the student's mastery of some phase. When weaknesses were found, the student was provided with remedial drill materials over the unmastered content. The student then took a final test to determine whether the remediation was successful. No student was allowed to leave one phase of the instruction until he had thoroughly mastered it. In the control group, the method of regular textbook lesson assignments and recitations was used.

The results of the studies indicate consistent gains in arithmetic achievement for the experimental groups over various periods of time. In one study, in a ten-week period the experimental group gained 1.41 years in arithmetic achievement as measured by standardized tests, while the control group gained just .40 year. In another study, over an entire year 35 seventh graders in an experimental group gained an average of 2.6 years in arithmetic achievement (range 1.1 to 4.0). Comparative gains for the control group were not reported.

The author concludes that the use of diagnostic examinations and remediation to individualize instruction is one very effective way to teach mathematics. He claims the method was effective because: (1) no pupil wasted time working on topics he had previously mastered; (2) the student did not have to wait for his whole class; and (3) no student left any particular topic until he had thoroughly mastered it.

D

Thornton, George R. , 1939
"A Factor Analysis of Tests Designed to Measure Persistence. "
Psychological Monographs, 51, No. 229.

The purpose of this study was to determine whether tests
purporting to measure the trait "persistence" were measuring the
same thing or whether there were several distinct variables being
referred to as one.

A battery of 22 tests was administered to 189 students in introductory psychology classes. Tetrachoric correlations were com-
puted and the results were factor analyzed.

Five factors emerged from the analysis. Two of these factors
seem to be variables closely related to the conceptual definition of
persistence then in usage. The first was composed of several tests
which appeared to measure ability to withstand physical discomfort.
The second, more closely related to our present conception of
persistence, was composed of four tests which measured either the
time spent on a learning task or the amount of productivity at a
learning task. The author characterizes this factor as "keeping
on at a task. "

We feel that this report provides us with evidence for a trait
called "persistence" and that it is distinct from involuntary inability to shift one's train of thought from simple endurance. Moreover, the frequency distributions reported by the author make it
clear that individual differences exist in this trait.

(W. J. W.)

F

Torshen, Kay, 1968.
"The Relation of Classroom Evaluation to Students' Self-concepts. "
Unpublished manuscript, University of Chicago, Department of
    Education.

The purpose of this research was to investigate the relationship of evaluation of cognitive achievement in classrooms to students' self-concepts. The two types of evaluation studied were
performance on a standardized achievement test and teachers'
classroom evaluations. Sears' Self-Concept Inventory measured
students' ratings of their own status in ten different aspects of
self-concept thought to be important at their stage of development.
The sample consisted of about 100 fifth-grade students of lower and
middle socio-economic classes selected from three school districts.

It was hypothesized that there would be a significant, positive
relationship between teachers' evaluations and students' self-

concepts, which would remain significant when the effects of objective achievement were removed. Because students get feedback about their achievement more frequently from teachers than from objective achievement tests, they may regard teachers' evaluations to be more relevant assessments of their academic competence. Teachers' evaluations may provide the basis for students' concepts of their own academic competence, even when there are considerable discrepancies between teachers' evaluations and objective test assessments.

The data indicate that there is a significant, positive relationship between teachers' evaluations of students' achievement and the students' self-concepts. Removing the influence of achievement test performance does not reduce the relationship significantly. However, the relationship between achievement test performance and students' self-concepts is not significant when the influence of the teachers' evaluations is removed.

These findings support the proposition that teachers' evaluations of students' cognitive achievement have a greater influence upon students' self-concepts than do their objective achievement tests evaluations. Further investigation of this problem is now in progress. In this larger study (involving 400 students) the relation of classroom evaluation and students' self-concepts to students' mental health is being explored.

(K.T.)

F

Torshen, Kay, 1969.
"The Relation of Classroom Evaluation to Students' Self-concepts and Mental Health."
Unpublished Ph.D. dissertation, University of Chicago.

The present study continues work described in Torshen (1968). It considers the relationship of cognitive evaluation to students' mental health. The students' self-concept was measured by self-reports. The analysis differentiated academic self-concept from nonacademic self-concept. Mental health was measured by teacher judgment on an overall rating as well as on a list of mental health symptoms. The sample consisted of about 400 fifth-grade students of lower, middle, and upper socio-economic classes selected from six school districts.

Analysis of the self-concept questionnaire yielded 12 distinct aspects of self-concept. The student's "academic" self-concept is more highly related to his teacher's evaluations ($r = .46$) than to objective achievement measures ($r = .33$). The relations of nonacademic self-concept to teachers' evaluations and objective achievement are close to zero.

Both measures of mental health show significant, positive
relationships to teachers' evaluations and objective achievement.
Teachers' ratings of mental health status yield correlation coeffi-
cients of .62 with teachers' evaluations and of .46 with achievement
test performance. The mental health symptom count shows correlations of .42 with teachers' evaluations and of .29 with objective
achievement. It is believed that the mental health symptom count
reflects less influence of teacher bias than does the mental health
rating. For this reason, more confidence is placed in the relationship involving the mental health symptom index. Of the symptoms
measured, those associated with intrapersonal distress (e.g.,
unusual fears, nervous tension, day dreaming, trouble concentrat-
ing) were most highly correlated with teachers' evaluations ($r=.43$),
achievement test performance ($r=.42$), and academic self-concept
($r=.32$).

These results indicate that students' academic self-concepts
and scores on mental health indices are positively related to objective test measures and teachers' evaluations of their academic
achievement. This relationship was found in all socio-economic
classes and at all normal intelligence levels. As in the 1968 study,
the relationships of achievement test performance to students'
self-concepts and to students' mental health was not significant
when the influence of teachers' evaluations was removed. The relationships between teachers' evaluations and students' self-concept
or students' mental health remained significant when the influence of
objective achievement measures was removed.

Self-concept and mental health appear to operate as distinct
but related aspects of personality. Correlations of the combined
aspects of self-concept and mental health range from .20 to .28.
Academic self-concept shows stronger relationships to mental
health (correlations of .26 to .39) than either nonacademic self-
concept (correlations of .08 to .11) or all self-concept aspects
combined.

(K.T.)

                                                                    E, G

Washburne, C. W., 1922.
"Educational Measurements as a Key to Individualizing Instruction
      and Promotions."
Journal of Educational Research, 5, 195-206.

Our interest in the paper centers on its description of one of
the key ideas behind an early attempt to individualize instruction
(the Winnetka Plan) and the effect of this idea on the use of class-

room time and evaluation procedures. This idea was that within
the curriculum, time should be the variable unit, whereas achievement should be the constant one.

The writer points out that previous curricula had been laid
out in terms of constant blocks of time. Within these time units,
the achievement of pupils varied according to the student's ability.
The Winnetka Plan, however, fixed achievement per subject matter
units and varied time to fit the individual capacities of the children.
Each child was required to master certain essential skills and
reach certain goals, but at his own rate of progress.

This idea made new evaluation procedures necessary. It
was essential to define which unit objectives must be mastered and
at what level before the student could go on to the next unit. It
was necessary to prepare tests which completely covered each
subject matter unit and diagnosed the difficulties of each child.
Finally, it was necessary to prepare self-correctional practice
materials which would at once prepare the child for the diagnostic
tests and enable him to make up the deficiencies shown by the test.

In sum, the writer argues that only when achievement replaces
time as the constant factor in the schools can instruction be individualized to meet the needs and capacities of the child.

E, G, F

Washburne, C. , Vogel, M. , and Gray, W. S. , 1926.
Results of Practical Experiments in Fitting Schools to Individuals.
Supplementary educational monograph, Journal of Educational
    Research. Bloomington, Illinois: Public School Publishing
    Company.

This book presents the results of a comprehensive series of
comparative studies and controlled experiments designed to evaluate the effectiveness of the Winnetka Plan. The comparative
studies contrasted the Winnetka schools with the schools of other
suburban systems and two special private schools. Comparisons
were made in such areas as the number of students making "normal"
progress, achievement in basic subject matter areas, and the
efficiency of the traditional class versus individualized instruction.
The experimental studies examined whether students learned more
or less rapidly in the individualized method and the effects of individualization on achievement. During the course of the survey
approximately 28, 000 tests were administered to gain the necessary
data.

Only some of the results can be briefly mentioned. First,
there were tentative indications that the Plan enabled more students
to stay up with the work appropriate to their age level. This is

attributed to the fact that the student could proceed at his own rate
and did not have to repeat an entire grade if he had difficulty in
some areas of the curriculum. Data are presented showing the
great disparities in the amount of work that students accomplish in
the conventional classroom. In the multiplication experiment, for
example, the best pupil in the class accomplished almost five times
as much work as the average students. The individualized program
also showed striking indications of variability in students' rates of
progress across subject matter areas. For example, in a comparative study in arithmetic performance, it was found that the
fastest student was almost two years ahead of the average students,
while the slowest student was approximately one year behind.

The results regarding achievement were equivocal. On the
one hand, when Winnetka's students were compared with students
from the other schools in terms of performance on standardized
tests in reading, spelling, language, and arithmetic, their achievement was on the average higher, except in spelling. On the other,
in the experimental studies the students learning under individualized instruction did not achieve more than those learning by the
traditional classroom techniques. It was pointed out, however,
that the individualized method did save students time, especially
for the faster children. In terms of later high school achievement,
freshmen form the Winnetka schools on the average outperformed
students from other elementary schools in English, mathematics,
and social science. They were outperformed in Latin only. Finally,
on the whole, the Plan allowed more time for the students to par-
ticipate in group and creative activities having potentially powerful
affective consequences.

                                                                    D

Weiner, B., 1965.
"The Effects of Unsatisfied Achievement Motivation on Persistence
      and Subsequent Performance."
Journal of Personality, 33, 428-42.

This study investigated the effects of continual success or
continual failure on the persistence of different types of students
at simple learning tasks. The purpose was to test the adequacy of
different models of achievement motivation.

Sixty male college students were given the McClelland T. A. T.
measure of need for achievement and the Mandler-Sarason Test
Anxiety Questionnaire. The upper and lower quartiles on the joint
distribution were employed in further study. Half of the students
in the experiment were told that 70 per cent of the college students
tested were able to complete the tasks within a specified time.

These students were then allowed to complete every trial before being told that time had expired (Success Condition). The other half of the students were told that only 30 per cent of the college students tested were able to complete the tasks. These students were then told that time was up on each trial before they could complete the task (Failure Condition).

The findings indicated that subjects high in achievement motivation persisted longer, i.e., undertook more trails, in the failure condition than they did in the success condition. Subjects in the lowest quartile on achievement motivation, on the other hand, persisted longer when they were placed in the success condition.

We feel that this study indicates the importance of success and failure as an influence on persistence. Without examining the problems of achievement motivation, there is some evidence that for at least some students a situation which enables the student to succeed leads to greater persistence. Which group of students represents the rule and which the exception is a matter of conjecture in the absence of a more inclusive experimental sample.

(W. J. W.)

E

Wright, William, 1967.
"Achievement as a Function of Time: An Analysis of Selected Stanford Achievement Test Battery Results."
Unpublished manuscript, University of Chicago, Department of Education.

This study investigated the relationship between subject matter mastery and time (grade level) for subtests of several of the 1964 Stanford Achievement Test Batteries. For each subtest a mastery level was defined according to the results of the battery's first administration as the score corresponding to the 80th percentile. The percentage of students achieving at or above this criterion score was plotted for each subtest as the test was administered over time to successive grade levels.

The resulting graphs for the several batteries indicated the following points:

1. A large percentage of students eventually attained the predefined mastery level.

2. Some students reached mastery faster than others.

3. The time it took for a majority of students to reach mastery varied for the different subject matter subtests.

For example, in the Intermediate Battery, 20% of the students reached the criterion score by the beginning of grade 5, while 60% or more of the students reached this point by the end of grade 6. These figures varied by subjects with the shortest time lag required for a majority of students to attain the criterion being found in Arithmetic Computation and the longest in Paragraph Meaning and Language. In the Primary Battery, 20% reached the criterion score by the middle of grade 2 while, in general, two-thirds or more reached this point one and one-half years later.

*   *   *   *

This study demonstrates that while the majority of children do reach a selected criterion level of achievement, they differ in the rate at which they attain this level. Similar findings hold true for most standardized achievement tests.

B

Yates, Alfred, and Pidgeon, D. A., 1957.
Admission to Grammar Schools.
London, England: Newnes Educational Publishing Company.

This report presents some results of a seven year inquiry into the efficiency of the procedures by which primary school students were allocated to secondary schools in England. The study focuses on the problems of allocating students to grammar or academic secondary schools, examines the validity of the assessment procedures in use at that time, and suggests a minimum set of requirements for sound methods of allocation using a number of pieces of information about the primary school student's academic potential.

Subjects for the study were two complete age groups of primary school graduates from one of England's boroughs. Approximately 1,200 students were graduated, but due to drop-outs the number of students for whom complete data was available was reduced. The students used in the analysis attended 15 secondary schools (seven grammar and eight modern). While in primary school these students had taken a battery of intelligence and achievement tests and had been rated by their headmasters for their academic potential. Two criterion scores for success in secondary school were used: a secondary school headmaster's assessment of the student (SHA) scaled for the student's ability and school examination marks (SIE) standardized and scaled with reference to a battery of examinations given by the borough's Local Education Authority.

A particularly important finding of the study was the

relationship between a student's verbal intelligence as measured by an intelligence test and his success in secondary school. While the primary headmaster's assessment (PHA) of the student was the single best predictor of success in secondary school as measured by SHA or SIE criteria, the verbal intelligence test was the single best predictor among tests and examinations used. It correlated .79 with the headmaster's assessment of the student (SHA) for the 1952 age group in their second year of secondary school and .73 for the 1951 age group in their third year of secondary school. Its correlation with school examination marks (SIE) was above .70. The authors suggest, too, that primary headmasters' assessments were based to a high degree on the student's verbal intelligence and ability.

These data, therefore, support earlier findings by the authors that while both tests of ability and tests of achievement are useful predictors of success in secondary school, a verbal test of intelligence or general ability is the best predictor.

*   *   *   *

These results suggest that <u>ability to understand instruction,</u> as measured by verbal intelligence tests, is an important determinant of level of achievement in secondary school.

E, A

Yeager, John L. , and Kissel, Mary Ann, 1969.
An Investigation of the Relationship between Selected Student
    <u>Characteristics and Time Required to Achieve Unit Mastery.</u>
Working Paper No. 46, University of Pittsburgh, Learning
    Research and Development Center.

Another study in a series examining the relationship between various learning rate measures and selected student characteristics is reported here. Earlier studies had found no relationship between the characteristics and the rate measures previously used under the Individually Prescribed Instruction (IPI) Program. This study hypothesized that there would be a significant positive relationship between the student's initial state of readiness to learn and the number of days he required to master a given task.

Data were collected in connection with the IPI program for eight samples of student performance. Each sample was taken from one of four mathematics units - - addition, subtraction, multiplication, and division - - at one of two criterion levels of achievement. The student's readiness to learn a given unit was determined by a composite consisting of the following measures: (1) the student's pretest score on the unit, (2) his I.Q. , (3) his

chronological age, and (4) the total number of units he had previously mastered. In addition, the number of skill to be mastered
in the unit was considered to be a student variable. The relationship between each of these variables and the number of days the
student needed to master the unit to the appropriate criterion level
of achievement was examined using simple correlational methods.
A regression analysis was also performed.

The results indicate that there was a significant positive
relationship between the student's state of readiness to learn and
the number of days he required to master a given unit. In particular, the student's pretest score, the number of skills to be mastered in the unit, and the student's age were highly predictive of
the time the student needed to learn (average correlations were
-.60, +.62, and -.43 respectively). I.Q. had little predictive
power, supporting earlier findings that it has little effect on progress in a program where the student proceeds at his own rate and
is capable of mastery at some time. The fact that the total number
of units the student had previously mastered in the program did
not have a consistent effect on the time needed to learn was contrary to all expectations and deserves further examination.

The authors conclude by suggesting that an index developed
from the five measures used in the study or from other readily
obtained measures on the student could be used to identify students
who might be expected to spend an excess amount of time on a
particular unit. Such an index might thus provide a means of
assessing relative student progress in a self-paced program.

*   *   *   *

Two of these findings are of special importance. First, the
student's pretest score, but not a generalized measure of his I.Q.,
predicted the rate at which he learned the appropriate mathematics
unit. This suggests that the student's relevant previous learning,
not his general ability to learn as represented by his I.Q., is the
key to predicting his rate of learning on a given unit. Second,
learning rate on a unit was affected by the number of skills to be
learned in the unit. This suggests that as learning tasks increase
in complexity and length, the variation in the rates at which the
students learn the tasks will also increase.

INDEX